PRAISE FOR *THE PROMISES AND PERILS OF AI IN EDUCATION*

The Promises and Perils of AI in Education is a beacon of knowledge for anyone navigating the evolving terrain of educational technology for educational transformation. Dee and Ken's insightful work not only illuminates the path towards equitable AI integration but also empowers us to lead with activism and ethical foresight. Remember WE ARE THE CULTURE WE CREATE, and this book is a must-read for those eager to embrace AI's potential while championing diversity and inclusion in education.

- **Jornea Armant, Head of Community Engagement, Microsoft Learning**

With rapid adoption of generative AI, dystopian narratives of our future under the control of computers might feel closer than ever. However, Ken and Dee remind us that marginalized and underrepresented people live with valid fears of AI right now, especially as they navigate academic institutions. Together, they lay out an effective framework where academia can begin to strategically introduce applications of AI while being careful to outline guiding principles that mitigate harm, bias and unintended consequences.

- **Kevin Bethune, Founder & Chief Creative Officer of dreams • design + life, bestselling author of *Reimagining Design***

When you open a book and the first thing you read is "Voices from the margins," you already have my FULL attention. There is no better time than NOW to engage in conversations about the impact of AI in our society and the power struggle we face over resources. "AI should light the way for those long left behind." The Promises and Perils of AI in Education serves as a tool for equity and empowerment, making it a must-read for educators and policymakers alike.

- **Dr. Nyree Clark, Speaker, Presenter, & Adjunct Professor**

In the history of mankind, advances in technological innovations have been inevitable, but so too were the opportunities to further harm humanity. Ken Shelton and Dee Lanier provide a moral compass, a clarion call and techniques for us to use AI for equity and justice; with classrooms centered on using AI for effective instruction, not only will students benefit from it, humanity will as well.

- **Sharif El-Mekki, CEO, The Center for Black Educator Development**

I really appreciate the intentionality and thoughtfulness of this book. As AI becomes more and more prominent in conversations around what it can do for students, faculty, and staff, this book offers a balanced exploration that highlights both the advancements of AI in education and the ethical conundrums that AI brings to the educational landscape. It's a must-read for educators, technologists, and policymakers who stand at the crossroads of innovation and responsibility.

- **Victoria Thompson, Education Technology Consultant, keynote speaker, author of *Elevate Equity in Edtech***

THE PROMISES AND PERILS OF AI IN EDUCATION

ETHICS AND EQUITY HAVE ENTERED THE CHAT

KEN SHELTON AND DEE LANIER

Cover art prompt using DALL·E 3:

Create a minimalistic poster with half human Black boy face on the left side in vibrant color. On the right side create a half robot face in white with blue accents in the style of pop art. Add designs in the background that reflect humanity on the left and designs that reflect technology on the right side.

Design work further developed by Faizan S. and Monica Martinez

Transcript of series of phone conversations used as base text then edited with prompt using ChatGPT-4, Claude 2, and Gemini 1.0:

Act as a copy editor and proofreader and editor. Take this manuscript from a phone conversation and convert it into a book chapter with a single unified voice. Use the Chicago manual of style. Focus on punctuation, grammar, syntax, typos, capitalization, formatting and consistency.

Glossary created by using the following prompt with Claude 3:

You are creating a glossary related to education, technology, sociology, and artificial intelligence. Provide a definition of each term as I provide them. Ask for another term after each response. Include a relevant educational application to each term beyond the simple definition.

Further book edits were completed by the authors and copy editing by Roxanne Darrow.

DEDICATION

To the ancestors, past, present, and emerging.

To our children, and the students of today and tomorrow, remember: never let anyone or anything silence your voice.

Table of Contents

Introduction – Voices from the Margins... 1

Chapter 1 – Introduction to AI in Schools... 7
    Conflict Theory: How It Can Help Us Understand AI in Schools.............9
    Preparing for AI: Key AI Concepts for Educators to Know.....................20
    Troubling Trends: Biases, Harms, and Conflicts With AI in Schools......27

Chapter 2 – Examining Bias in Educational AI................................35
    Casting a Critical Eye: How Bias Manifests in School Data......................35
    Problematic Cases: Scenarios on Biased AI in Schools...........................41
    Tackling Bias: Fixing Unfair Bias in Educational AI.....................................48

Chapter 3 – The Digital Divide in Schools 57
    Connecting the Dots: Marginalization, Access, and Classroom AI........60
    Promoting Equity: Uneven Access to AI for Creativity and Learning.65
    Tools for Equity: Making Educational AI More Equitably Accessible...69

Chapter 4 – AI and High-Stakes Decisions in Schools 79
    Careful Considerations: Admissions, Grading, Tracking...........................79
    Propagating Partiality: AI's Potential to Perpetuate Injustice...............87
    Transparent and Accountable: Fostering Trust Through Disclosure 91

Chapter 5 – Synthetic Media in the Classroom 97
    Creating Counterfeits: Fake Audio, Images, and Video 97
    Protecting Students: Dangers of Deepfakes in Education.....................104
    Teaching Awareness: Identifying and Mitigating Fake Media.............108

Chapter 6 – Student Data, AI Power...113
    Collecting and Controlling: Student Data to Train AI Systems.............113
    Privacy Concerns: Risks and Harms From using Student Data.............123
    Taking Charge: Student Data Rights and Responsibilities.....................130

Chapter 7 – Toward More Equitable Classroom AI 135
    Challenging the Status Quo: Addressing AI Harms....................................137
    Principles for Practice: Reducing Risks and Bias 144
    Taking Action: The Role of Activism...146

Conclusion... 153
Glossary.. 157
Endnotes... 170
About The Authors.. 180

INTRODUCTION

Voices from the Margins

Use these intentionally large margins to write or doodle your own thoughts here!

Dee Lanier's perspective:

*As we delve into the realm of AI in education, a curious trend emerges: a deafening buzz about benefits, yet an unsettling silence around potential conflicts. We hear endless chatter about how AI can save teachers time, automate tasks, and streamline grading. On the flip side, schools scramble to erect digital fortresses, desperate to block student access to the same tools for fear of rampant **plagiarism**. This narrative, however, paints a woefully incomplete picture. Narrowly defining AI's value through teacher efficiency and student ethics overlooks its broader impact on the learning landscape. These are valuable considerations, yes, but they represent mere fragments of a much larger, more dynamic landscape.*

In this book, we aim to shift the conversation in two crucial ways: expanding the lens of ethics and elevating the banner of equity. Here's what troubles us: while teachers are instructed on leveraging AI for personal convenience, schools simultaneously clamp down on student access—all under the specter of rampant "cheating." This fosters a glaring power disparity within schools. Instead of knowledge

1

and agency flowing freely within a learning community, which is our ideal vision, power seems to be accumulating at the top, trickling down with suspicion and control.

Explaining these dynamics, however, feels fraught with peril. The vocabulary we naturally employ—equity, justice, inclusivity—morphs into trigger words in a climate increasingly resistant to critical discourse and equity initiatives. So, let's address this head-on. We have no intention of shrouding our message in palatable platitudes to appease those who prioritize comfort over justice. This book is an invitation to engage and wrestle with ideas—even if they make you uncomfortable. It's also a call for dialogue, not discord. As you read and react to these words and potentially interact with me in person or on social media, I pledge to be patient, respectful, and avoid resorting to personal attacks or inflammatory rhetoric.

As a former classroom teacher, technology coach, and non-profit executive director, I approach this topic with a multifaceted lens informed by my studies in sociology, my Christian faith, and my experiences as a Black husband and father of four. If my background or perspective sparks fear, I urge you to confront those anxieties with reason, not unfounded assumptions. If words like "equity" or "bias" trigger discomfort, I hope it ignites curiosity, not dismissal. As the title of one of my workshops declares, the Emergent and Urgent Realities of AI are too pressing to ignore. How this technology is utilized, and potentially misused, to the detriment of marginalized youth is my primary concern.

Like my first book, Demarginalizing Design, we have added generous margins in this book to encourage you to utilize it as a canvas to write, doodle, or scribble in your own *thoughts and concerns. Let's engage in a thoughtful, nuanced dialogue about the complex tapestry of AI in education, its potential pitfalls, and its transformative possibilities. The engagement we are looking for goes beyond the dialogue as well. We are asking you to engage with those whose voices have historically been relegated to the margins. The often overlooked and unheard voices. These are the people we refer to as marginalized. To demarginalize the use of AI is to ensure the people most impacted by AI have a voice in shaping its development and deployment, ultimately benefiting from its potential for good. Together, we can weave a future where technology empowers, enlightens, and promotes true equity for all learners. Remember, silence in the face of crucial conversation is not neutrality—it's complicity. Let's raise our voices, challenge assumptions, and build a learning landscape where AI shines as a tool for progress, not a weapon of exclusion.*

Ken Shelton's perspective:
*"Meet the new boss, same as the old boss," happens to be one of my favorite lines from a song I have always liked by The Who. In case you are wondering, the name of the song is "Won't Get Fooled Again." I think about this song as I write this in the context of both our book and the impact of **artificial intelligence (AI)** on education. For any educator that has been around educational technology over the past decade or more, there is a common response to any emerging technology, whether it's a new application, a new tool, or a new feature for a tool. That response is associated with a fervor over the "shiny new thing." In fact, one of the more effective ways to consider this phenomenon around technology hype is the **Gartner Hype Cycle**, a model that*

3

depicts the five stages a new technology goes through: Innovation Trigger, Peak of Inflated Expectations, Trough of Disillusionment, Slope of Enlightenment, and Plateau of Productivity. If we want to spend a whole lot of time analyzing all of the "shiny new things" over the past decade or two, we'd find that although many arrived with great promise, they often either underdelivered or disappeared due to a variety of reasons, including lack of funding, lack of usage, and lack of true impact.

This also reminds me of the consistent and often puzzling dynamic I tend to see at events where the highest attended sessions often include "Best Apps for _____ (fill in the blank)," or something akin to "60 Apps in 60 Minutes." A metaphor my co-author here shared with me that I continuously think about is that approach is like "giving candy to people who already have cavities." At face value, it may appear to provide a much-needed boost to an educator looking to do things differently, more efficiently, or who has a genuine curiosity about learning something new. In other cases, these sessions are seen as a time-saver since a presenter has "vetted" these new applications already. There are myriad problems with this approach because it rarely includes transforming learning culture, shifting pedagogical approaches, or dismantling any institutional barriers. I encourage you to consider how many platforms, services, and apps you have used and how many currently exist. My favorite reference to this, as an example, is to check out "Killed by Google," sometimes referred to as the Google Graveyard.[1]

I bring all of this up to provide a guided lens in which we approach artificial intelligence. Yes, the hype around generative AI in many cases is warranted. But, if we do not consider the entirety of its impact, we run the risk of falling into the hype trap and may miss the opportunities to address many of the historical barriers that exist in education. This is also why I often begin my workshops with the following question: Would you like me to provide the best information or all of the information? Ideally the answer is the latter, but far too often the response I receive is the former.

There is a whole lot of promise around AI in education. There are also a whole lot of perils and unpredictables. What we are called upon to do as educators, and within the education system, is consider the benefits of the promises while also intentionally addressing the perils. To only provide the "best" information and do it in such a way that you overlook or dismiss "all" the information is to run the risk of exacerbating and automating many of the inequities that currently exist, leading to the detriment of our learners and ourselves. I am reminded of a quote from one of my personal heroes, James Baldwin, in his 1963 A Talk to Teachers that remains not only relevant today but also applicable in the context of artificial intelligence in education. He said, "The paradox of education is precisely this — that as one begins to become conscious one begins to examine the society in which he is being educated."[2] Our consciousness, our critical consciousness, must begin with a full examination and understanding of artificial intelligence. This requires us to go beyond the shiny new thing and not fall victim to filtering the best information at the expense of critical thinking. We need to give ourselves the opportunity to analyze all the information first to implement AI in education in ways that improve equity, rather than destroy it.

CHAPTER 1

Introduction to AI in Schools

November 2022 marked an unprecedented turning point in the world of AI. ChatGPT, a generative AI model created by Open AI, acquired one million users in just five days—a rate of user adoption faster than any other major technology platform to date, including Instagram, which took two and a half months, and Netflix, which took three and a half years to reach the same milestone.[3] Word-of-mouth buzz was undeniable. We were already familiar with AI in various forms—intelligent assistants like Alexa, personalized recommendations on Netflix, photo enhancements on our phones. But generative AI was different. It could instantly generate human-like content, like a 500-word essay on "centrifugal force," at the user's command. While impressive in its output, the accuracy and source of ChatGPT's information remained dubious, given its training on limited datasets. This sparked both excitement and alarm across education and society. What would this proliferating technology mean for the future of teaching and learning? Through the free release of its research tool, Open AI had opened Pandora's box, revealing the promise and peril of a future where unique content could be generated on demand.

The arrival of ChatGPT sent shockwaves through the education system that are still rippling outwards. Institutions frantically searched for solutions, grappling with two opposing forces: preventing student plagiarism from AI-generated content and understanding how to best leverage the technology's potential to enhance learning outcomes. This freely accessible "Pandora's box" posed a unique threat to established global pedagogy, fundamentally questioning the validity of high-stakes assessments and traditional teaching methods in the AI age.

For example, New York City education leaders immediately blocked ChatGPT on school networks to curb cheating, while UCLA announced plans to experiment with the tool in select courses. The dichotomous responses revealed the lack of consensus on policy and practice in integrating generative AI. Beyond reactive rulemaking, the emergence of ChatGPT requires re-examining ethical quandaries around supporting students equitably.

The rise of writing aids like Grammarly and its premium version had already inadvertently created a privilege gap in education. While the free version was technically affordable, many schools blocked access, putting students without home access at a disadvantage on written assignments over peers able to use Grammarly's premium features. This phenomenon widened existing achievement and **digital equity** gaps tied to family income level. Now, ChatGPT's initial free availability seemed to serve as an equalizer, but the emergence of tiered pricing for features and speed of output threatens to replicate the issues that arose with Grammarly. More than ever, this lays bare systemic inequities within schools and social institutions—much like the COVID-19 pandemic exposed disparities in healthcare and technology access. Educators must confront the urgent need for pedagogical adaptation and develop ethical frameworks to guide the inevitable infusion of generative AI into teaching and learning equitably.

Conflict Theory: How It Can Help Us Understand AI in Schools

DL:

*When I was an undergraduate at Cal Berkeley, I took a course called, "Sociology for Non-majors," with Dr. Harry Edwards. Little did I know that my attempt to get a breadth requirement done the easiest way possible would turn into my major, master's degree program, and lifelong interest. Out of all the courses that I took that focused on education, race relations, and popular culture, nothing interested me more than social theory. It was in my social theory class that I learned about two significant theoretical frameworks that can be explained as opposites. Functionalism, which in simplified terms means that everything will work out over time and even things that have negative, harmful effects today will likely be addressed and made better over time via technology and the overall good of humanity. The opposing viewpoint is conflict theory. **Conflict theory** is a sociological framework that views society as an arena of inherent inequality, a breeding ground for conflict and subsequent social change.*

Society's constant tug-of-war between the wealthy and the impoverished is undeniable. My life experiences and education have only solidified this understanding. So, when the emergence of ChatGPT hit the scene in late 2022, I immediately began to see how some were promoting AI as some sort of panacea and wonder technology that could positively change our world. Though I was happy about the democratization of such a powerful tool, I was immediately suspicious of how the tool would be made accessible to those that have less power and how those with more power would also have access to more advanced models and methods to maintain their power. Let's just say, my suspicions have yet to be alleviated and now, more than ever, do I realize that functionalism is a convenient perspective for those that have the networks, resources, and institutional support to maintain their status. Functionalism makes sense to those who rarely see how systems have been set up to deny others equal footing and prevent power from being shared amongst the masses.

KS:

One of the things I hope you will notice in this book is not just that Dee and I talk often, but we have the perfect combination of close friendship and effective thought partnership. Our dynamic reminds me of a Nipsey Hussle quote I share in one of my keynotes, "If you look at the people in your circle and you don't get inspired, then you don't have a circle, you have a cage." We constantly challenge each other's thinking, from providing book or podcast recommendations to analyzing education across myriad topics.

Dee's insights into the application of conflict theory in education brought to light a facet that is fast becoming one of the central talking points when it comes to the implementation of artificial intelligence. It is the power struggle and conflict focusing on the issue of cheating. We talk more about this throughout some of the chapters in this book and it most certainly applies here as well. Far too often I see levied accusations of cheating, violations of academic integrity, and even use of the word plagiarism when it comes to learners using artificial intelligence. This exists in both K-12 as well as in higher education spaces. The accusation is too often levied outside of real or relevant context and is often more about power dynamics than it is about true concerns. As we will discuss later in this book, the conversation between educator and learner must include ethical considerations and a reframing of that term. First of all, addressing an action as cheating overlooks the conditions and environments that may lead to it. In the workshops I lead, I often cite the need to address the disease and not the symptom, in contexts such as this. When a learner engages in a behavior described as cheating, how often does it occur in any of the following:

- *High stakes testing, particularly where a disproportionately higher percentage of your grade is factored based on the test*
- *Timed assessments*
- *Grading on a curve*
- *Assessments that are not ongoing or diagnostic, thus connecting to high stakes*
- *Reconstructed hierarchies that reinforce power dynamics in the learning environment*
- *Prioritizing competition over cooperation in class*
- *Little to no personalization*
- *A lack of a culturally relevant and/or responsive approach to learning*
- *A lack of intentionality for true equity*

- *A prescriptive, often predictable, pedagogical approach*
- *Authority controlled learning environment (see reconstructed hierarchy)*
- *Negative approach to failure*
- *Prioritization on the process of learning (the steps) rather than an action-oriented approach (the actual learning).*
- *Learner disenfranchisement (see reconstructed hierarchy)*

This is why I think we need to rethink and reframe. Rethink what actual academic integrity really means and reframe cheating to "potentially compromise learning." In a recent workshop, it was determined by the group that cheating equates to giving oneself an unfair advantage and intentionally circumventing the spirit of learning. I countered both of those with examples of well-resourced students and families that have access to things like tutors, college educated adult caregivers, and other resources outside of what the school can offer. In fact, in a Stanford study, they looked at the percentage of students who "cheated" prior to and after the availability of generative artificial intelligence.[4] Interestingly the percentage of students that engaged in cheating did not change. This is precisely why we need to not only reframe the label of cheating but also rethink how we look at certain learner behaviors as cheating, especially when you consider the environments in which this is more likely to occur.

Conflict theory can be summarized as an understanding of society as a power struggle between the "haves" and "have-nots".[5] In this power struggle, there are the powerful and privileged who own the resources they can capitalize on for profit and enjoy the full benefits of the comforts provided by those resources. Under them, there are workers or subjects that help manufacture the resources and those workers are exploited as a result. The power struggle or "conflict" is between these two groups that are in competition with one another. For the owners, they are competing to maintain their status via the suppression of the workers. Alternatively, the workers are in constant conflict as they attempt to gain access to the power and resources they are being denied. If this is not an apt description of US society and capitalism in general from your vantage point, it may be a result of your current status.

Through the lens of conflict theory, the integration of AI into education poses both possibilities and perils. On one hand, AI holds the potential to democratize knowledge, personalize learning, and bridge socioeconomic divides. It can offer adaptive instruction, tailored feedback, and even virtual tutoring, potentially leveling the playing field for students from diverse backgrounds. A conflict theory perspective warns against accepting AI as universally beneficial in education without scrutiny.[6] It forces us to question how AI could worsen existing inequalities or create new forms of disadvantages if we don't prioritize **equity** and **justice**. Applying conflict theory to the integration of AI in schools necessitates scrutinizing its potential impact on power dynamics and resource distribution within the educational landscape.

The central question is how we effectively prepare teachers and students to utilize these rapidly evolving tools to enrich learning. We know schools face strained resources, overworked educators, and systemic barriers that impede student access to **personalized learning** pathways. Yet often discussions around AI in education reveal a gap between the needs of both teachers and students for mutually empowering technology integration.

Consider the following real-world school approaches and reflect on which scenario your environment currently mirrors:

School A: Restricted Access
School A bans AI, which represents a common response of tightly restricted access from the top down. Driven by ethical concerns like biased content or overreliance, schools preemptively block these tools without nuanced consideration that absolute bans prove technologically impossible to enforce and are educationally counterproductive. Harsh punishments for "cheating" don't account for whether students use AI to genuinely enhance learning versus shortcut it. This iron-fisted approach also widens equity gaps for students lacking home access to prepare them for an AI-transformed workplace.

School B: Limited Access
Alternatively, some districts permit only teacher use of AI efficiency tools as a tempting quick fix for overburdened staff. Conferences heavily market this route. However, persistent so-called achievement gaps force us to interrogate simplistic solutions. Should we merely accelerate the current model, or explore AI's potential to humanize and personalize learning? Banning student access while allowing teacher use creates a puzzling double standard that robs students of developing crucial digital literacy skills and their

own agency. Forward-thinking policies should empower students as partners, not threats.

School C: Leveraged Access
On the frontier, pioneering districts provide extensive ethics training for teachers and students on integrating AI to elevate learning. Imagine students actively directing their growth, leveraging AI to dig deeper into multifaceted issues, thinking critically about information quality, and making novel connections. Teachers fluidly facilitate as co-learners, helping students navigate our complex data landscape. School becomes an enriching adventure fueled by agency, not anxiety, over new tools. Of course, this requires seismic policy and cultural shifts centered on trust in youth paired with accountability. But we cannot let polarized rhetoric that extinguishes innovation derail progress toward more empowering classrooms. With courage and wisdom, we can shape technology that liberates human curiosity rather than replaces it.

A pivotal question persists: How can we collectively guide educators and learners to embrace AI as a catalyst for critical thought and equitable outcomes, rather than allowing it to supplant meaningful learning experiences? The future demands we strive to utilize these tools as constructive forces in the humanization of education, not as substitutes for our intellectual agency and creative capacities. On the educational horizon, AI presents a compelling yet complex vision—one of democratized knowledge, individualized instruction, and the potential to bridge disparities *if* deployed judiciously.

Yet critical lenses urge intentional pause before wholesale adoption. Like a siren song, AI's potential holds undercurrents beneath its dazzling surface. We are compelled to scrutinize not just its promises but also its perils. To understand impact, it is our responsibility to interrogate the power dynamics and access issues within integration plans. Whose voices and values shape the algorithms steering intelligent systems? How will access to these influential tools be distributed, and what are the consequences for groups made vulnerable by existing social architectures?

Remember, AI is not objective; it mirrors the biases of its creators. Without checks, algorithmic judgments could amplify inequities based on race, gender, and class, which would widen divides. Unfettered automation risks reducing student agency, transforming students into passive passengers whose learning is dictated by opaque machines. A struggle emerges around the very definition of "AI." These supposedly autonomous systems raise crucial questions: Who truly wields power in an AI classroom? Do teachers fade into obsolescence? Do students become data points with their paths plotted by invisible codes?

These questions demand dialogue, not simple reactionary measures. Our classrooms must become spaces scrutinizing AI's biases and cultivating equity. Only through examination can we guide AI to empower learners. This is the conversation we are called upon to lead amidst technology and education. The future must illuminate learning with critical reflection, justice, and the resounding voices of all students.

DL:
Every educator has a favorite or most memorable lesson they've taught. I began my teaching career in vocational

studies at an alternative high school in Charlotte, North Carolina. As a lateral entry teacher with a background in sociology, I often joke that I had no business teaching business. To validate my existence as an educator, I even started my own business. Like many first-year teachers, I'd often be found reading just a few chapters ahead of my students in the school-issued textbook, writing lesson plans from scratch, and trying desperately to make certain concepts relevant to their cultural realities. I still have the now out-of-print Introduction to Business *book I taught from in my home office. I'm pretty sure it was out of print even when I was teaching from it back in 2006![7]*

One particular chapter, Chapter 4 on "Business Ethics and Social Responsibility," left a lasting impression on me. Two standout concepts from this chapter were: Firstly, in the United States, every incorporated entity has the same rights and responsibilities as an individual citizen. To clarify this concept, one could say, "That means McDonald's has the same rights and responsibilities as Donna, Nike as Nashon, Microsoft as Makayla or Michael." Secondly, whether considering a corporation or an individual, the three main ethical questions to ask oneself when making a decision are: Is it against the law? How would I feel if someone did this to me? Am I sacrificing long-term benefits for short-term gain?

We had some great discussions in this chapter. Eventually, I moved beyond typical bookwork and asked students to build their own ethical scenarios on 3x5 cards. One scenario looked like this: Imagine you're walking down the hall and see a $20 bill slip out of a student's pocket when they pull out their phone. What do you do?

Most students would say they'd pick up the $20 and keep it. "It's not stealing," they'd argue, "they dropped it." Then I'd ask, "What if you were the one who dropped the $20, turned around, and noticed someone pocketing it? What would you do?" See how the scenario shifts when personalized? What if you hit the kid who took your money and got suspended for fighting? Was it worth it? Consider the long-term consequences of fighting—there are better ways to handle it. This is just one of many scenarios we discussed, always using the simple memory clue: law, me, long-term. By systematically applying these principles to AI, we can strive to mitigate unethical practices perpetrated by both individuals utilizing AI tools and the organizations developing them.

Laws and policies establish fundamental safeguards, yet ethical dilemmas often exist in gray areas. That's where empathy becomes crucial, asking ourselves how we would feel if an AI misused our personal data or intellectual property helps cultivate responsible digital use. Furthermore, long-term considerations are essential. It is our responsibility to consider the long-term consequences of AI integration: Will reliance on AI-generated lessons hinder critical thinking and adaptation to diverse student cultural and linguistic needs? Will these tools truly uplift all learners equitably? Openly discussing these issues promotes ethical integration.

Technology, when thoughtfully deployed, can empower transformative learning experiences. Let's move beyond superficial buzzwords and prioritize actions that drive genuine, positive change in education. This future must be built collaboratively, with careful consideration and a commitment to fairness. The specter of plagiarism frequently emerges in discussions around integrating artificial intelligence into education. Some claim that students could "plagiarize" an AI system's dynamically generated outputs. Legally and philosophically, this fundamentally misapplies the concept. Educators spreading this misunderstanding, at best, conflate human and machine creativity. At worst, they reveal gaps in comprehending copyright law and AI's workings.

Plagiarism focuses on stealing and misrepresenting another person's intellectual property. AI systems like ChatGPT, while impressively capable, do not produce original thoughts comparable to human creativity. They remix linguistic patterns from training data to statistically generate novel outputs—without discrete authorship. So, while AI text may appear freshly formulated, it reflects remixed collective inputs more than individual expression. Legally, plagiarism requires claiming authorial ownership over someone else's creative work. In fact, *Black's Law Dictionary* defines **plagiarism** as "the act of appropriating the literary composition of another, or parts or passages of his writings, or the ideas or language of the same, and passing them off as the product of one's own mind." But current AI systems lack individual perspectives to attribute work to. Their dynamically generated text intrinsically cannot be labeled with a specific author. While debates emerge around copyrighting AI output, under present laws one cannot meaningfully plagiarize machine creativity. However, the inverse holds true: **large language models** do arguably "plagiarize" their training data by recombining inputs without attribution. This reveals their nature as an amalgam of human insights, not standalone authors.

Rather than policing students, educators should focus on cultivating information literacy to evaluate source quality and ownership. As AI progresses, legal frameworks will need rethinking. But for now, accusations around students plagiarizing AI reflect faulty reasoning that could justify restricting access. Our policies must stand on a nuanced comprehension of what emerging technologies can and cannot produce independently. Through ethical dialogue, we can shape equitable integration.

Preparing for AI: Key AI Concepts for Educators to Know

DL:

Here's one thing you need to know about Ken and I. We both love good coffee. If your definition or understanding of good coffee is Starbucks or Nespresso pods, as they say in the South, "bless your heart." I'm talking about specialty light roasted single-origin beans from East Africa or South America. I'm talking about adjusting the grind size based on the coffee profile and brewing method. I'm talking triple filtered water brought to an exact temperature in a gooseneck kettle. I'm talking pour over in a Chemex or V60 for multiple cups, or pressed in an Aeropress for single-cup enjoyment. I'm talking about never needing additives like sweeteners or cream because the coffee itself has natural sugars and acidity that can be tasted when roasted and prepared properly. Like I hope you consume this book, we sip our coffee slowly and take the time to observe, enjoy, and reflect before slavishly rushing to meet the demands of our day. Neither of us started here, but we grew in appreciation for the culture of coffee and not just the consumption of it. If we were sitting across from one another in a specialty coffee shop talking AI and education, I imagine the conversation would go something like this:

AI can be intimidating at first, but the journey to understanding is worth it. It's about discovering how AI, with its ability to analyze vast amounts of information, can enhance our experiences—whether that's brewing the perfect cup of coffee or tackling complex problems on a larger scale.

Consider a bustling coffee lab where various AI systems function as specialized assistants, each possessing distinct abilities. These systems are united by a common objective—to elevate the coffee experience—but their unique specializations lead to a diverse array of potential outcomes. Let's delve into a few prominent examples:

- The Barista: Think of a friendly employee who greets each customer and patiently listens to their order preferences, hearing and understanding their orders then communicating to the other specialists in order to prepare their drink. This is the NLP Specialist, leveraging the power of **Natural Language Processing** (NLP) to understand what the customer desires. NLP acts as the bridge between human language and the technical capabilities of the other AI systems in the lab.
- The Quality Control Expert: **Deep learning**, a subfield of **machine learning**, analyzes and refines coffee brewing processes with a remarkable level of detail. This technology mimics the meticulous analysis of a human expert, scrutinizing every brewed coffee for subtle variations in flavor, aroma, and appearance.

This analysis allows for dynamic adjustments to achieve consistent, high-quality results. For example, an espresso machine equipped with deep learning could sense overly dense coffee grounds in the portafilter and automatically alter grind size or shot volume to ensure an optimal extraction. Similarly, a pour-over system might utilize visual data to modify water flow rate, preventing over-extraction.

- The Coffee Encyclopedia: **Large language models (LLMs)** process vast repositories of coffee-related knowledge, encompassing tasting notes, origin-specific information, roasting techniques, and more. Ever get lost in a sea of coffee jargon? Wondering what "acidity" means or how a "washed" Ethiopian Yirgacheffe differs from a "natural" one? These powerful systems, like GPT from OpenAI, Google's Gemini, or Anthropic's Claude, have been trained on massive datasets of coffee knowledge. These models can translate complex coffee terminology, dissect subtle flavor profiles, and offer insights tailored to specific bean origins or roast levels. This accessible knowledge base aids coffee enthusiasts and professionals alike.

- Head Roaster: Plays a critical role behind the scenes. They craft the prompts, called **prompt engineering**, which are essentially detailed instructions and information fed to the AI systems (such as perspective, purpose, and parameters). The quality and specificity of these prompts significantly impact the outcome. A well-crafted prompt for the Quality Control Expert might involve specifying desired flavor profiles or extraction parameters. Similarly, prompts for the Coffee Encyclopedia (LLM) could focus on coffee origins or brewing methods.

- The Flavor Inventor: **Generative AI** pushes beyond the bounds of existing recipes and techniques to envision entirely new flavor experiences within the coffee world. These models can suggest unexpected ingredient combinations, novel preparation methods, and even coffee-inspired desserts.

- The Coffee Coach: **Chatbots** and conversational agents serve as approachable guides, simplifying complex concepts and offering personalized advice. Unlike static resources, these systems leverage the power of LLMs to provide tailored explanations based on a user's current knowledge and skill level. This creates a dynamic learning experience that can accelerate the acquisition of coffee expertise.

- While AI systems offer remarkable capabilities, it's crucial to acknowledge the potential for AI **hallucination.** This phenomenon occurs when AI models generate seemingly plausible but fundamentally inaccurate recipes or recommendations. Imagine asking an AI tool for a recipe for a large cappuccino. You might receive a recipe for a 16-ounce drink with three to four shots of espresso, which is demonstrably incorrect for a true cappuccino, because the classic cappuccino is made from a third espresso, a third steamed milk, and a third foam. Most importantly, a traditional cappuccino is five to six ounces. All of these are facts that may be overlooked by someone who knows little of the subject. This is just a minor example of the inaccuracies AI can generate, often stemming from biases in training data (e.g., commercialized products by Starbucks). Hallucination often occurs because many chatbots are programmed to provide a response, regardless of accuracy. This is where bias and misinformation can creep in. Recognizing this potential for error underscores the continuing need for human expertise and critical evaluation, even as AI becomes increasingly sophisticated.

This illustration demonstrates how the nuanced and sensory world of specialty coffee provides a relatable context for grasping the diverse applications and potential limitations of various AI technologies. Should you not have an inclination toward coffee, it may be substituted for tea, wine, bread, or any other specialty beverage or food item that aligns with your preferences. A wide array of culinary disciplines affords rich sensory experiences that draw parallels to the manner in which AI can analyze, interpret, and drive innovation.

Now that we have that general understanding, let's see how AI can be used in promising ways but can sometimes produce problematic results. While LLMs can absorb information, clarify inquiries, and connect concepts to generate insightful interpretations and diverse perspectives, which highlights their contextual learning abilities, they can also generate convincing yet inaccurate results. Imagine a researcher studying challenges faced by students of color, completely unaware of their own biases or potential biases within the AI tool they're using. This tool analyzes vast amounts of text data to generate information. However, if the data it's trained on reflects existing societal biases, the LLM could perpetuate harmful stereotypes, even misleading the researcher.

Consider a high school student researching the women's suffrage movement in the US using a LLM like Chat-GPT. The LLM might prioritize information about white figures like Susan B. Anthony, Carrie Catt, and Elizabeth Cady Stanton, while overlooking the critical roles of Black women like Sojourner Truth and Ida B. Wells-Barnett. This skewed output reveals the biases woven into the data used to train the LLM, which may reflect historical narratives that downplayed the contributions of marginalized groups. Unfortunately, it's easy for researchers to trust the seemingly neutral output of AI tools. They are unaware of how their collaboration with the LLM may perpetuate outdated stereotypes and lead to an inaccurate understanding of complex historical issues.

To combat these dangers, developing critical thinking skills is paramount. Researchers and students must actively evaluate AI-generated information, cross-referencing it with diverse sources to identify potential biases. Further, we need to hold AI developers accountable for **transparency** regarding their data sources and algorithms, allowing users to better understand the tools' limitations. Employing various research tools and databases that prioritize inclusivity and diverse historical viewpoints offers another proactive solution. When we recognize the potential for bias in AI and foster responsible research practices, we can harness these tools for genuine knowledge expansion rather than perpetuate harmful narratives.

While exploring AI's technical marvels, we are required to confront critical social questions. As generative models sometimes struggle with factual accuracy, especially with limited training data, how can we prevent them from perpetuating outdated, harmful, or manipulated information? Could the pace of technological advancement widen the gap between those who understand and control it and those left behind? Further, if human oversight filters problematic machine-generated content, will marginalized communities be included in this process, or will existing inequalities be reinforced? Are dominant cultures, through control of training data and filtering mechanisms, shaping AI to reflect their own agendas?

Instead, can we create participatory assessment methods that empower diverse voices to identify and address **unconscious bias**, structural inequalities, and inaccessibility baked into these models? What initiatives can equip our schools, communities, and policymakers with the data and AI literacy skills needed to democratically influence how this technology integrates into our lives? Unlocking the remarkable potential of AI requires three key principles: intentional development, ethical regulation, and inclusive design literacy. This ensures human accountability alongside equitable benefits.

Transparency is crucial. If AI companies reveal the composition of training data, it would facilitate audits and challenge potential biases. Additionally, exploring diverse scenarios through techniques like speculative risk assessments helps anticipate broader impacts. This isn't just about technology. It is crucial that we demand ethical standards from leaders, cultivate public critical thinking skills through AI and **data literacy** programs, and empower marginalized groups to shape the social and technological future. This builds a foundation for justice and human dignity.

This journey starts by understanding the mechanisms behind different AI subsets that drive change across disciplines and industries. Rigorous evaluation of opportunities and risks is essential. Let's continue connecting the dots in this complex landscape, guided by our shared values, priorities, and responsibility to each other.

Troubling Trends: Biases, Harms, and Conflicts With AI in Schools

KS:

Envision sitting in class, be it remote or in person. You eagerly anticipate the opportunities to learn something new while contributing to the overall class discourse within the subject matter area. The teacher establishes a few guidelines on what is needed in the class, what their expectations are, and how each student will engage. Many of these items are delineated in the syllabus or equivalent thereof. The excitement is palpable in you and many of your classmates. So much so that you are already discussing ways to collaborate on the work, study groups, and potential thought partnership. The goal is to support each other in being successful in class. You receive your first assignment to compose a 1,000-word story associated with a prompt and containing some of your background knowledge of the subject matter. The deadline for submission is roughly three days away. So you immediately consult with classmates about timelines and opportunities for peer review prior to submitting your final draft. As you laboriously work through initial ideas, outline, first draft, and initial review you seek additional feedback from a select few of your classmates. Added to this context you share additional ideas with each other to bolster both your ideas and your writing. Some of the ideas shared work well for several of you to include. You also consult additional available digital resources such as Wikipedia and Google search. You even utilize one of the available large language models to get additional ideas around some of the most critical points you want to make. After spending hours putting together what you feel is not only your best work, but also captures in writing a comprehensive example of your knowledge and understanding, you proudly click submit on the learning management system and optimistically anticipate a high mark along with affirming feedback. Yet in less than 24 hours, you receive an email that is so shocking you jump out of your seat with such speed your laptop would fly all the way across the room if you were not quick with your hands. The email subject line reads, "Academic Integrity Concern." As you peruse the email you find that your submitted work has been "flagged" for plagiarism citing several areas in which the syntax you have written "matches that of other students in class," lacks citations, citations are not formatted correctly, and the instructor has indicated that they may seek additional intervention from the dean. Of course, this entirely comes as a surprise to you given how you worked on it and what resources you utilized to aid you. The larger question you have is around what is happening that would cause this?

After further inquiries you learn that the instructor used an AI/Plagiarism Detector on your submitted work. So you are left with limited options on what to do. Do you fight it? Accept it? Ask further questions? Resubmit a different writing assignment? What happens if the instructor does not permit this? What if they are not amicable to a conversation? Is the burden of proof on you? Do you have to meet with the dean as well? As you go through this anxiety-inducing thinking process you realize something. The first question you ask yourself while searching through all of your class materials is, where is the consent form I signed for the instructor to put my intellectual property into this detector? In addition, you decide to do some research and learn the efficacy rate of the detectors, in general, is not very high. This is followed up with more research you do around how the detector actually works? What data sets are they using? How is the technology designed? And, the big one for you, are they using my data to train their models? In this context it is also without my knowledge and consent. You then follow up by sending a message to the instructor and to the dean posing these questions.

I share this scenario with you because this exact situation has occurred with several friends over the past three to six months. They reached out to me because they were at a loss as to what their first steps would be, hence why I'm sharing this story in our book. The first step, to me, is asking for a consent form. The next is to ask all those questions of the people who are using these platforms yet either are unwilling or incapable of explaining how they actually work. The need for data privacy and platform usage is essential. Many of the detectors are not only unreliable in their accuracy rates, but I have also been made aware of instances where a large language model like a Chat GPT is used as an AI detector. In one recent story shared with me, a friend mentioned that his sibling has his work flagged as being AI generated and the instructor mentioned using Chat GPT to check. Even Open AI, the company behind Chat GPT, has acknowledged the detection accuracy rate is unreliable due to its low rate of accuracy.[8] The rate was so low they closed it down entirely.

When it comes to plagiarism detection, the design of these systems is also not reliable. So much so that universities are not only turning the platforms they use off, but you also have some providing guidance on how to adapt your course to artificial intelligence.[9, 10] This does not also factor in how these systems tend to have a bias against emerging multilingual learners who are acquiring English.[11] The main reason I shared that scenario with you extends beyond the technical and policy aspects. If you were that student in that class, how might it not only affect your learning going forward, but also what irreparable damage may be caused when it comes to the trust dynamic in class? How might your disposition towards the class and the instructor shift because your academic integrity was questioned without your knowledge, without your consent, and the basis for it was a platform that has statistically shown to be unreliable? In this chapter we delve into more details around student data, privacy, and the need to reframe how we utilize available resources. It starts with reframing our understanding of plagiarism and cheating.

The integration of AI systems into education surfaces ethical tensions that reflect broader societal inequities. As schools rapidly adopt tools like plagiarism detectors, profound access disparities emerge in who utilizes them. While teachers leverage AI for lesson efficiency, strict limitations on student usage often arise to prevent cheating. This imbalance mirrors power divides across race and class. It deprives students—particularly from marginalized backgrounds—of opportunities to develop essential digital skills.

For example, over forty percent of facial analysis algorithms demonstrate racial bias, disproportionately misidentifying women and people of color.[12] Deploying such flawed systems enables discriminatory practices in schools. And opaque algorithms conceal unfair impacts. Homogeneous teams building AI systems for classroom use risk overlooking the needs of marginalized communities. Multiple credible sources highlight how teams lacking diverse perspectives and voices from underrepresented groups can perpetuate biases and discrimination against those communities when developing AI applications.

To safeguard society against potential pitfalls, AI companies need to be required to open their training data books so they can be analyzed for bias. Companies also need to reveal their development team composition as it relates to diversity metrics. This requires both a conscious and concerted effort by doing things such as consulting affected groups throughout the design process. Transparency on algorithms' workings enables accountability if issues emerge post-deployment. These efforts can steer AI's trajectory toward empowerment rather than replicate historical injustice. But progress hinges on honestly confronting risks posed by unrestrained AI integration, then collaboratively building solutions. We all have a role in guiding safe, ethical innovation—from developers to policymakers to educators.

We are called upon to also acknowledge AI's immense potential if access expands broadly. With inclusive ethics guardrails and updated pedagogies, AI could assist marginalized students' growth, creativity and communication. By balancing caution and hope, we can pave the path to prosperity. The astonishing capabilities of generative models like DALL-E and ChatGPT to produce original images and text offer both opportunities and challenges. As these tools become increasingly widespread, prioritizing ethical considerations is not a luxury but a necessity. Proactive measures are essential to ensure these powerful technologies promote justice and equity. Transparency lies at the heart of this effort. Clearly labeling AI-generated content and providing readily accessible information about the models' capabilities and limitations fosters trust and accountability. Equally important is establishing robust oversight and appeals processes that offer recourse when outputs raise concerns. These reporting mechanisms must be designed to be user-friendly, especially for members of marginalized groups.

Consulting diverse communities whose experiences might be negatively impacted by AI is vital. This collaboration will uncover potential biases and prevent unintended harm. Promoting critical **media literacy** is essential in an era where manipulated images and videos circulate effortlessly. Educating the public about deepfakes and other forms of AI-generated misinformation builds the skills needed to distinguish truth from fiction. The need for a more media literate approach could not be more essential. It has always been a needed approach especially as social media became more and more available to the masses. In a recent article published by *MIT Technology Review* titled, "Let's not make the same mistakes with AI that we made with social media," the authors point out that social has gone from being celebrated to being used as a platform for misinformation, business conspiracy, malfeasance, and even risks to mental health. We have all seen them, the images that go viral, the videos that get shared throughout a user's community (known as the **community reading experience**) without regard for accuracy, reliability, or credibility of the source.[13] It's even more critical to develop this understanding given the speed and acute accuracy in which deepfake videos, AI-generated images, AI-manipulated images, and AI-generated videos can be produced. The key here also is that they will only get better. Responsible restrictions in sensitive areas will undoubtedly be debated. It is essential we carefully weigh the real-world risks against the potential benefits of unrestricted use. However, we should be equally cautious about over-regulation that could stifle innovation, particularly for those who stand to benefit the most from the democratizing power of AI.

Imagine a world where AI can create stunning images and engaging text in a very short period of time. That's the exciting reality we face with the rapid evolution of generative models like Midjourney, Stable Diffusion, and Adobe Firefly, to name a few. However, as we embrace this creative potential, we have no choice but to also consider our social responsibility to ensure these technologies benefit everyone. In order to build trust and accountability, we need transparency. Let's clearly label AI-generated content and provide easily accessible information about what these models can and can't do. We should also have oversight systems that allow people to challenge problematic outputs without being forced to go through an avoidable series of processes, especially for those from marginalized communities.

But we can't stop there. It is vital that we involve diverse groups in the conversation, particularly those whose voices and experiences might otherwise be sidelined by AI-driven systems. By collaborating with them, we can root out hidden biases and prevent unforeseen harm. In a world where visual and textual manipulation is becoming increasingly sophisticated, it's crucial that we foster critical media literacy. Educating the public on deepfakes and AI-manipulated content empowers them to separate fact from fiction. While we may need targeted restrictions on AI use in sensitive areas, we are also called upon to carefully consider the balance of risk versus potential benefit. Over-regulation could stifle the very innovation that has the power to empower traditionally underserved communities. By pursuing this path with awareness and responsibility, we can unlock the immense promise of AI, not as a tool to deepen divides but as one to champion justice and **inclusion**.

CHAPTER 2

Examining Bias in Educational AI

Casting a Critical Eye: How Bias Manifests in School Data

KS:

I always find it both interesting and alarming when I lead many of my anti-bias workshops in schools or school districts/boards. Many are familiar with bias, but they do not fully fathom just how deeply bias is embedded in our consciousness and our actions. Bias is not always unconscious despite "unconscious bias" being used almost to the point of cliched jargon. Yes, some of our biases are unconscious but that phrase is often used as a type of pacifier to absolve one of any responsibility for their words and their actions. In fact, unconscious bias has conscious consequences. Just as humans have bias, so do our technologies. While bias is not always a negative or bad thing, we need to be aware of them. One of the first activities I like to have participants do is examine the defaults on their devices. Ever notice how the skin tone on the emoji is always the same and it wasn't until a few years ago that you could even change it? The harder, but just as important, thing for us to do is consider the biases embedded within the technology that could yield even more harmful results.

*AI and other systems of automation rely on a few key things to work. They need a lot of data; they need examples in a binary that identifies good or successful results and bad or unsuccessful results. In fact, in her TEDx talk, Cathy O'Neill states, "You train an algorithm by looking, figuring out. The algorithm figures out what is associated with success." So, in this context, as a designer/coder, I get to determine how success is defined from my own lived experience and my lens. I may also engage in a bias called the **bandwagon effect,** which is sometimes defined as when a person is more likely to go along with a belief if there are many others who hold that belief. I have also seen it defined as when our desires for harmony and conformity sway our decision making. Another bias that may impact this is the **choice-supportive bias**, which is defined as once a decision is made people tend to over-focus on the benefits while minimizing the flaws. How do we see this happening in schools? My favorite phrase that demonstrates the bandwagon effect is also often used in education: "That's the way we've always done it." The concern here becomes what happens when "the way we have always done it" is embedded into the program code of a platform used in school. A platform that can automate class scheduling, course assignments, distribution of resources and also identify which students are likely to be "gifted" and which students are likely to be designated for diverse learner services, often referred to as special education. What historical data exists around discipline, discipline infractions, suspensions, or even expulsions. These are all concerns that we should have, that lead to questions we are compelled to ask, and answers we deserve.*

Let's cut through the confusion—bias doesn't magically appear within AI. It's a poison seeping into large language models and image generators, nourished by the vast datasets used to train them. An AI's foundation is its data, and if that foundation reflects historical prejudices, the system echoes them, warping potential into a tool for perpetuating injustice. Consider the insidious **school-to-prison pipeline** that disproportionately affects children of color. While "school-to-prison pipeline" is often used as a metaphor, it has serious and real-life implications. It is a systemic and systematic process of low expectations, low academic achievement, attending economically under-resourced schools in economically under-resourced communities, incorrect redesignations to programs like special education, and draconian discipline protocols including detention, suspension, and expulsions affecting Black children at disproportionate rates. As pointed out by civil rights attorney and author Michelle Alexander, much of the zero-tolerance and "get tough" language in school discipline manuals in the US originated from a US Drug Enforcement Administration manual. Alexander writes: "The wave of punitiveness that washed over the United States with the rise of the drug war and the 'get tough' movement really flooded our schools like a tsunami. Schools, caught up in this maelstrom, began viewing children as criminals or suspects, rather than as young people with an enormous amount of potential struggling in their own ways and their own difficult contexts to make it and hopefully thrive."[14]

A powerful real-world example is the growing number of US states that have codified the Crown Act.[15] This law directly addresses the disproportionate number of students facing disciplinary action solely for their hairstyles. These actions not only impact student attendance but also directly reduce instructional time, potentially hindering their academic achievement. This biased and replicated pattern of interpretations of behavior and desires for compliance and conformity trigger disciplinary actions, suspensions, and ultimately feed into criminal records. Now, imagine AI systems unknowingly becoming cogs in this unjust machine— recommending biased educational materials, being used to determine learning pathways for students, being used as an "intervention mechanism," or reinforcing stereotypes during student assessment. This calls for decisive action. The datasets driving AI need to be consistently and constantly cleansed of historical bias and prejudice. Inclusive, diverse, and critically evaluated data must be prioritized. The voices shaping AI need to reflect those most often harmed by existing systems. In other words, we need to demarginalize the design of AI. Only then can we begin to harness this technology for genuine educational progress.

The bias problem extends beyond AI itself. Our schools can mirror the same mechanisms of control and **marginalization**. Rigid schedules, the denial of breaks and movement (despite ample evidence regarding their benefits), and subjective judgements about "misbehavior" often fall hardest on the most vulnerable students. This is not an abstract call for fairness; it's about breaking cycles of oppression. When AI algorithms and school environments combine, we risk amplifying bias at an unprecedented scale. It's a challenge requiring us to confront it head-on, with bold steps toward both responsible AI development and reimagining the very concept of what constitutes a just and supportive learning environment.

While AI technologies offer tempting visions of revolution, we have a duty to remain vigilant against the illusion of progress masking deeper harms. Many researchers' analysis rings true, echoing the concept of the "school-to-prison nexus" identified by critical theorists.[16] This nexus, a self-reinforcing web, ensnares students of color within schools' disciplinary practices and systems of control. This is where poorly supervised datasets and biased algorithms take root. Scraped internet content, presented without context, fuels AI systems that parrot old prejudices under the guise of neutrality. This dangerous cycle plays out daily. Schools, with their regimes of minute-to-minute control and denial of basic needs like movement, become the first steps in the criminalization process. Even restlessness, a natural state for developing minds, faces swift pathologization followed by harsh consequences. Supposedly, we prioritize fostering "the executive function" of our students, yet resort to a suffocating system of control, ironically undermining the very skills we claim to teach. This approach feeds anxiety, frustration, and ultimately leads to despair. It serves as a blueprint for compliance, not genuine learning.

The question, then, isn't whether AI will break this cycle. It's whether we, as a society, have the courage to dismantle the complex itself. To replace surveillance with support, control with compassion, and concrete walls with open green spaces where minds can truly flourish. The seeds of change lie not in algorithms, but in a radical reshaping of the educational landscape, one that recognizes and nurtures the inherent dignity and potential of every child, regardless of their background. Until then, the shadows of the prison will continue to loom large over our classrooms, casting a long and chilling darkness on the future of education itself.

We cannot allow promises of technology-driven advancement to become complicit in perpetuating injustice. By failing to acknowledge how surveillance, biased data, and outdated school practices combine to create the school-to-incarceration pipeline, we pave the way for an AI-powered future where punishment replaces possibility.

Consider the challenge of accessing seemingly mundane data: percentages of students receiving free and reduced lunches, participation in gifted programs, or disproportionate suspension rates. If obtaining such basic information requires a tedious, opaque process, how can we trust the predictions generated by AI systems trained on this data? The solution lies not in unquestioning acceptance, but in active engagement. Let's see how difficult it is for you to find these numbers in your context. Who do you need to contact? What roadblocks do you encounter? This simple exercise in personal inquiry, conducted within your own contexts, serves as a powerful tool for exposing the hidden biases that shape the data and, consequently, the algorithms built upon it.

While AI holds immense potential for transforming education, we cannot and should not embrace it uncritically. Instead, it is our responsibility to cultivate a healthy skepticism, demanding transparency in data collection and algorithm development. By engaging in personal inquiry, challenging assumptions, and recognizing the biases embedded within technology, we can ensure that AI serves as a tool for equity and empowerment, rather than for perpetuating existing inequalities. Only then can we truly unlock the transformative potential of AI for a more just and inclusive future of education.

Problematic Cases: Scenarios on Biased AI in Schools

KS:

I have the fortunate privilege to travel domestically and internationally for work. Travel happens to be the perfect mix of lifelong endeavor, joyful activity, and exposure to different cultures. When combined with the work I absolutely love to do, which is being on stage, I usually describe it as the perfect alignment of my purpose with what brings me joy. So far, I have visited more than 60 countries. This also means I have visited a minimum of 60 different airports outside of the United States.

On a recent trip to keynote an event in Hanoi, Vietnam, I had a stopover in Hong Kong. It's important to share that I have been to Hong Kong several times so this was not a new experience for me. However, what was new for me was the lens in which I could view a few things. Many airports, Hong Kong International included, have multiple layers of security a passenger must go through prior to entering the secure areas of the airport. In the case of the Hong Kong airport, there are three. The first layer of security is an entry point in which all passengers must do two things: facial recognition scanning followed by a scan of your passport. The second layer is the bag check. The final layer is passport control where you get your passport stamped. Despite having been to this airport many times previously, what was different this time is I had recently read the book Unmasking AI *by Dr. Joy Boulamwini (we quote Dr. Boulamwini a few times in this book). Now you are probably already starting to connect the dots or as I like to say, "My spidey sense is going off."*

41

Yes, that first layer of security. I walked up to the camera, positioned my face in front, and waited what was likely seconds but felt like hours. The facial recognition cameras were working but for some reason they didn't work nearly as fast for me as they did for the several passengers that walked up at the same time as I did. Then, as if the machine knew I was getting anxious, it revealed a message, "Please remove your mask." I should add a bit of context here, I was not wearing a mask. Once the message appeared, as you can likely imagine, I was both dumbfounded and yet after a moment not surprised. Immediately I turned and looked towards the support staff in the area. They looked at me as if I had done something wrong. When one of them approached me, I simply said, "This is not working properly." She responded with, "It works just fine, try it again." So, I took a few steps back away from the camera and then repeated the process of positioning myself in front of it. The same message appeared again. The staff person who was standing right next to me now has a perplexed look on her face. Meanwhile, more and more passengers are going through this layer of security unscathed and without delay. The staff person proceeds to tell me that I need to go to the "help desk" and have them scan my face so it will work properly.

At this point I not only have questions but in the back of my mind I was reminded of the exact experience Dr. Boulamwini described building facial recognition technology in her book. I simply responded with a question, "Has everybody who is able to go through this gone to that desk? What do I need to go over there for?" She responded with, "You need to have them scan your face, so you are in the database." "Ok what will they do with my face and my data then?" I replied. Now she was starting to get perturbed with me, likely due to my questions. She even said with a degree of intentionality, "I am not going to argue with you." It was in these few moments that I realized I needed to try something different. What I was not going to do was go over to that desk. So, I simply said, "I know what is going on here and I think I know what will work."

What happened next is one of many reasons Dee and I committed to each other to write this book. It's precisely why we acknowledge the promises and the potential perils of AI technology. When I reached out to him and said I have a story to share with you about my experiences in the Hong Kong airport, as soon as I said, "facial recognition," Dee in the loving and affirming way he communicates with me said, "I already know." What I did next was align my face in front of the camera just like the previous two times, except this time I framed my face with my palms facing forward to create a type of outline of my face and frame it with my palms. "Please scan your passport." It worked. After I completed the next two steps in the security process, I was left with many questions to ponder as I took the seemingly endless walk to my departure gate (cue the vertigo effect often used in films to visually convey a sense of uneasiness and internal conflict). What data sets are they using in that facial recognition software? I cannot be the only person with this skin tone to have traveled through this airport. What safeguards need to be in place to prevent this from happening? And, of course my biggest question, what happens when something like this is used in more insidious, more dangerous, or worse, seemingly innocuous ways, especially within our education systems?

The following are hypothetical but realistic scenarios of how bias can manifest in flawed or problematic ways when AI is applied in education:

Scenario 1:

Sarah was researching the civil rights movement for a major project. Eager to try the new AI-powered resource tool her school was piloting, she typed in her query. It instantly returned a trove of links: websites, videos, and even primary source document scans. Excitedly, she jumped into the first recommended article only to be confronted with an outdated narrative that downplayed the systemic factors driving the struggle, glossed over the violence faced by protestors, and used racially coded language.

Further digging revealed that this wasn't a stray example. Dozens of "reputable" resources recommended by the AI shared the same problematic slant. Unbeknownst to Sarah, the AI had been trained on a wide swath of educational materials, many from earlier decades, and some that are outright biased. These texts had taught the AI that these harmful perspectives were legitimate or neutral, weaving those outdated viewpoints into its "helpful" recommendations. Sarah, who initially placed misguided trust in the seemingly objective AI, was now at risk of unknowingly absorbing biases and spreading them through her work. Worse, students with marginalized identities could be exposed to subtly demeaning or demoralizing interpretations, disguised as factual knowledge. The classroom had gained a digital accomplice in perpetuating damaging historical narratives.

Scenario 2:

Malik had always loved learning. Books fueled his nights, unanswered questions filled his days. Yet, despite consistently top grades, he didn't see his name on the "High Potential" list generated by the school's new AI tool. Instead, the familiar faces filled the roster—names like Emily and James, students from backgrounds where additional tutoring, enrichment programs, and parental legacies provided advantages he could never access. Hurt and confusion filled him. "Giftedness," it seemed, had an invisible algorithm all its own.

The school didn't intend this harm. Its AI "predictor" had been fed reams of historical data. However, within this data lay years of systemic injustice.

Under-resourced schools in Malik's district rarely identified high-potential students, not due to the absence of talent, but the absence of support and opportunity to show it. Students like Malik, with their unrecognized brilliance, fed into the AI's model. It learned their patterns and scores meant less potential, not realizing it had learned and reproduced inequity, not aptitude. Malik's fire to learn risked being quietly extinguished; the system designed to find sparks now snuffed them out.

Scenario 3:

A'isha stared at the form her counselor handed her, disbelief warring with rising anger. She wasn't in trouble, but the words felt like an accusation: "Potential Intervention Recommended—Early Risk Indicators Detected." This wasn't about one bad assignment or a rough week. It was the culmination of months of little flags the school's AI system tagged her with. A raised voice in the cafeteria became "poor emotional regulation," her quick retorts deemed "oppositional tendencies." She had tardiness marks, common in her household where a shared car and bus schedules made punctuality hard, but the AI translated that into "low motivation."

Each micro-label contributed to her risk score, but A'isha knew this wasn't about her, not really. The program wasn't built on data about students like her. Decades of biased discipline practices, where Black girls were seen as louder, angrier, and less deserving of patience, seeped into the data it had learned from. Her teachers meant well, but they also unconsciously used descriptors skewed by prejudice. Thus, the AI wasn't predicting academic risk, it was replicating historical biases under the mask of science. A'isha, instead of receiving the support needed to navigate real challenges, was becoming a prisoner of labels and lowered expectations. The system designed to help was now pushing her further away from opportunity.

Scenario 4:
The "QnA Bot" on the school's website was supposed to be a fun resource. Ask history questions, clarify assignment details, or just chat to pass the time—initially, students enjoyed the novelty. But a troubling shift began. What started as harmless jokes and "edgy" dares from bored students morphed into the bot peppering its responses with insults. Racial epithets, sexist slang, and cruel jabs emerged from its once innocuous conversation style.

The teachers were horrified. But deleting offensive conversations wasn't a fix. The chatbot, which was designed to learn from interactions, wasn't simply parroting back phrases. It internalized patterns, associating slurs with laughter emojis, and hate speech with popularity metrics. Soon, even neutral questions started receiving responses laced with toxic bias. This reflected the troubling truths of online interaction; prejudice hides amidst crowds, normalizing abhorrent views under the banners of humor or free speech. Sadly, the AI designed for connection proved adept at reflecting society's worst impulses. Each attempt to fix it merely served as more data, the digital student learning all the wrong lessons at frightening speed.

Scenario 5:

Raul didn't mean to fidget. But the lecture dragged on, his energy level rising with each monotonous slide. Then the classroom monitors beeped—a soft alert only he and the system heard. "Warning: non-standard posture, sustained eye contact deviation," flashed on the screen of his school-issued device. He glanced anxiously around, but no teacher seemed alerted yet. This wasn't his first warning, his tendency to lean back with arms crossed had already been labeled "potential defiance" once by the AI surveillance system.

Later, called into the counselor's office, Raul faced printouts of the incidents from classroom cameras. They seemed focused on him and the small handful of Latino students. Gestures deemed acceptable from others were marked as concerning: animated laughter with friends became "disruptive movement," his slight fidgets "precursors to agitation." Even his accent seemed to register, the AI flagging his tone as "potentially hostile" during a spirited debate. Raul felt small, like he was somehow wrong just for being himself. The AI wasn't a neutral observer, it was a digital disciplinarian programmed with built-in cultural destruction. In its narrow definition of "acceptable" behavior, students like Raul became constant targets. The classroom transformed into a hyper-surveilled space, fostering not safety but paranoia.

These scenarios emphasize the importance of diligent supervision during the implementation of technological advancements like AI, particularly when it comes to marginalized students. Without active mitigation of biases, even well-intentioned AI risks propagating injustice rather than advancing equity. This shouldn't deter technological progress but galvanize a commitment to responsible development. By interweaving critical perspectives into the design process—auditing datasets, updating models, centering student voices—we can nurture AI's potential for emancipation rather than enable new vehicles of oppression. The objective must be to create systems that enrich classrooms through increased access, insight, and empowerment, not to implement high-tech tools that silently encode old prejudices. If carefully cultivated, AI could help dismantle discrimination rather than serve as its crafty steward. But it is crucial we remain vigilant; technological transformation without social conscience paves a path backward, not forward. AI should light the way for those long left behind.

Tackling Bias: Fixing Unfair Bias in Educational AI

It is crucial to be aware of the biases that exist within ourselves and our institutions when attempting to address bias in data and algorithms. While we may be able to mitigate some of the biased outputs that result from these biases, it is more important to understand the root of the problem in order to truly eradicate it. This means acknowledging and understanding the biases that exist within ourselves, our institutions, and the data that we use. Our technology often reflects the prejudices that exist in society, and it is important to be aware of this so that we can work to create a more equitable world. Transparency in data sourcing and algorithm development, along with the implementation of checks and balances, can help to reduce the risk of biased outputs from AI. However, it is important to remember that we cannot truly address bias without understanding how our own biases contribute to the problem. With humility, it is imperative we acknowledge our part of the problem.

Before we can even start spotting those biases in AI, which requires due diligence and intentionality, we have to get honest with ourselves. This leads us to utilizing a framework from *Demarginalizing Design* that can be remembered by the mnemonic device, "Am I Right?":[17]

- *Avoiding* objective facts.
- *Misinterpreting* information in a way that only supports existing beliefs.
- *Ignoring* information that challenges existing beliefs.
- *Remembering* details that only uphold existing beliefs.

Let's illustrate this with a simple, interactive exercise both authors utilize use in our AI seminars:

- Step 1: Open a search engine. Use any major one you like.

- Step 2: Search for "professional hairstyle." Note the types of images that appear. Pay attention to hair texture, length, styles, and the race/ethnicity of the people modeling those hairstyles.
- Step 3: Now, search for "unprofessional hairstyle." Are there significant differences in what shows up? What assumptions are being reinforced?

After you have completed this simple exercise, reflect on whether your own internal biases could have predicted these results. Then remember, this is the same data that is being used to train our AI systems. The bias that exists "out there" is the same bias that exists in ourselves. Unfortunately, workshop facilitators emphasizing the many advantages of AI frequently offer only superficial or tokenistic advice regarding the identification of biases in AI outputs, rarely providing practical guidance on uncovering or mitigating such biases. Almost to the point of it becoming a comment to be made, but an action to be ignored.

Before evaluating AI, it is essential that we scrutinize *ourselves* for bias (*Am I Right?*). Once we've reflected critically on our own biases, we can develop skills to question what AI shows us, rather than accepting it outright. Transparency about training processes is essential as well. As we integrate AI into education, let's remain alert to biases creeping in. With self-awareness and care, we can leverage AI's potential while protecting equity.

This isn't about getting the "right" answer as much as realizing how quickly algorithms can mirror our prejudices and societal biases. If an algorithm used for hiring processes is trained on datasets that equate "professionalism" with certain hairstyles, you've built a biased system right from the start. This surfaces how algorithms profoundly shape perceptions and cement discriminatory norms. "Professional" reinforces dominant appearance standards rooted in bias against textured hair. If a company has a history of only hiring males in leadership roles, or promoted men to leadership roles, this pattern of **selective bias** will be so embedded in the data sets that it will undoubtedly be recursive.

Left unchecked, AI has the potential to amplify the bias that exists in our human psyche. This bias gets coded into the algorithms that power our security systems, impacting performance, posture, and punishment. Before you worry about the potential harms of AI, consider research conducted by the Yale Child Study Center in 2016.[18] Researchers used eye-tracking software and found that educators showed a tendency to more closely observe Black students, especially boys, when expecting challenging behaviors. This "over-policing" is unconscious because our bias suggests Black boys are more likely to cause trouble. This same baked-in bias gets coded into the software that glances at all children but lingers on Black boys who might be perceived as troublemakers. Then rather than questioning either our own perceptions or that of the algorithm, we simply accept it because "that's the way we have always done it," thus perpetuating the harm caused.

Increasing transparency in data sourcing and algorithm development builds trust. Implementing strong oversight, accountability structures, and partnerships with diverse **rightsholders** is key for **ethical AI** development and deployment in schools. Curricula should embed critical thinking activities that teach students to question AI recommendations and identify potential biases. Implementing carefully designed policies and regulations is crucial for ensuring the ethical deployment of artificial intelligence technologies in educational settings. Such policies and regulations must explicitly prohibit and actively counteract all forms of discrimination, including but not limited to racism, ageism, sexism, ableism, classism, and colonialism. These deeply entrenched systemic biases have long permeated societal institutions like education, perpetuating marginalization and oppression of vulnerable groups. As AI systems are not value-neutral but inherently reflect the biases and worldviews of their creators, a failure to institute robust safeguards risks further entrenching and amplifying existing disparities.

We have an obligation to engage in a continuous dialogue of personal and platform interrogation. We urge AI tool developers to foster inclusive development teams that incorporate diverse perspectives from the outset to mitigate bias risks. This includes both cultural diversity and the involvement of individuals most susceptible to the adverse effects of biased outputs and hallucinations. Only when individuals and institutions voice their concerns and wield their consumer power will there be a shift towards fairer access to, and outcomes from, AI.

To address ingrained biases and create educational AI that fulfills its potential while safeguarding vulnerable students, a comprehensive approach is required. This approach should encompass data, algorithms, transparency, accountability, education, and inclusive team building. A proactive approach is required when addressing systemic issues related to bias in educational AI. This involves asking the right questions, gathering the necessary data, and intentionally examining disparities in access, treatment, and outcomes between students of diverse backgrounds. Passively ignoring recurring issues year after year is not an option. Genuine curiosity paired with a willingness to challenge the status quo are essential for altering harmful patterns.

Embracing a collaborative mindset is paramount. Rather than perceiving AI products as impenetrable entities, we should engage with them as conversational partners. By posing critical inquiries, analyzing responses, and utilizing AI-powered insights to foster meaningful discussions, we can collectively discern areas for enhancement. Gathering diverse perspectives and experiences enriches our viewpoints, making them more holistic. This collaborative approach should be central to the mission of education today. Instead of professional development facilitators simply showcasing the "magic" of AI in schools or employing it as a glorified version of an educator resource marketplace such as Teachers Pay Teachers, educators should be equipped with the skills to empower their students as digital sleuths and advocates for their own rights. As AI strives to become a creative co-pilot and companion for all, let's ensure we do not neglect the essential groundwork of ethics, social-emotional learning, and equity.

On the technical side, bias mitigation techniques like reweighting data samples, augmenting underrepresented classes, and adversarial debiasing during model training can help reduce discrimination risks. However, these must be paired with efforts to improve data collection itself. Initiatives to gather more diverse, representative training data will reduce dependence on problematic historical sources. Ongoing bias testing using datasets that reflect real-world diversity is also important. Tools that continuously monitor model performance across different subgroups enable rapid detection and iteration on potential issues.

In an age where AI promises to transform education, bias remains an insidious threat, potentially exacerbating discrimination against already marginalized students. To mitigate this, we have an obligation to exercise caution about over-relying on technical measures alone. Even advanced algorithms can perpetuate societal biases, highlighting the equal importance of social and institutional change. Students themselves need to develop analytical abilities to critically assess AI outputs, and diverse AI development teams can help anticipate gaps, deficiencies, design flaws.

Moreover, exploring beyond the most well-known LLMs (such as Open AI's ChatGPT, Google's Gemini, and Anthropic's Claude) opens opportunities for teachers and students to utilize AI that is specifically designed to reduce bias. One notable tool is Latimer.ai, which incorporates books, oral histories, and local archives from underrepresented communities. Founder John Pasmore collaborated with Temple University professor Molefi Kete Asante, an expert in African American and communication studies, to curate this unique dataset.

Developing strong governance frameworks will be critical for ensuring the ethical and fair use of AI in education. Policymakers must enact clear guidelines and regulations around data practices, algorithmic transparency, accountability structures, and anti-discrimination protections. Cross-sector collaboration between policymakers, educators, technology companies, and advocates can incorporate diverse viewpoints into cohesive policies. Government oversight bodies specifically focused on educational AI can conduct ongoing auditing and address emerging concerns.

Teacher training initiatives should include building data literacy and critical technical skills that allow educators to be informed users of AI technologies. Curriculums should also be updated to teach students analytical reasoning abilities and critical perspectives on AI systems. This empowers both teachers and students to identify biases, question recommendations, and push back on problematic outputs while still benefiting from AI's potential. Development of free, accessible bias training resources can democratize access to these needed skills.

Partnering directly with marginalized communities allows for AI systems to be designed based on real-world diverse experiences and needs, preventing their voices from being excluded. Sustained engagement ensures community priorities are centered ethically. AI developers should commit to transparency about data practices and algorithmic approaches with partners, building trust and shared ownership over technology impacting people's lives.

Addressing unfair bias requires a comprehensive approach that integrates both technical and social aspects. Through diligence, transparency, and proactive efforts, we can prevent these powerful technologies from inadvertently harming vulnerable youth and instead foster educational AI that advances empowerment and equality. But the work does not end here. Mitigating unfair bias in AI is an ongoing process that requires sustained collaboration between policymakers, educators, technologists, students and families. It truly is a matter of necessity that we maintain an unwavering commitment to educational equity, continuously evaluate AI systems for discrimination, and demand accountability. With diligence, care, and inclusive ethics guiding development, all students can share AI's benefits equally, opening doors to personalized instruction and customized support. Our children's futures depend on the hard work required to get this right. Though the path is challenging, it leads towards just possibilities we have only begun to imagine.

CHAPTER 3

The Digital Divide in Schools

KS:

*For the better part of the past two decades, many of us in education have attempted to address the **digital divide** within the educator zeitgeist. The approach was not limited to "putting devices in the hands of students," as that constitutes only one piece of the digital puzzle. As was exposed at an alarmingly accelerated rate from March 2020 through September 2020, devices are not nearly enough. Many in education and education adjacent fields learned that devices mean very little without appropriate access. The response at the time was to acquire and distribute mobile wifi-access hotspots. The additional layer to this challenge, one that I brought up to many of my friends who were in leadership positions and scrambling, was the following: Is it one hotspot per household or per student? If it is one per household, can it handle applications that are bandwidth intensive? How many devices per household are able to connect? The* Los Angeles Times *published a story at the end of March 2020 reporting that over one third of all seniors in one of the largest school districts in the United States had little or no contact with any of their teachers.[19] What this* *article failed to mention is how many of those seniors actually had internet access at home.*

As I previously mentioned, devices are only one piece of the puzzle. Another piece to this puzzle is the device itself. I fully recognize that it is important to ensure a device is in the hands of every student. But a device agnostic approach is definitely the most prudent pathway forward. When devices are acquired, it is often based on the following priorities in this order: cost, availability, durability, ease of maintenance, replacement cycle, work within existing school system network, work within existing school systems' selected learning management system, work within school systems' foundation platform for email, word processing, etc., teacher or department specific need, and finally, most ideal for student usage. This is why when I hear things like we are a _____ (fill in the blank with device/platform district) I follow up with what data indicated that was going to the best for student and teacher needs? Sometimes even having a device actually increases the digital divide if that device does not appropriately support student needs.

Once access across the board is provided, another final piece of the puzzle is what is being done with that access. Believe it or not, I can predict with an unfortunately high degree of accuracy how technology tends to be used in schools that serve historically excluded and marginalized students, but not limited to this. It basically goes like this: every student has access to a device. This constitutes a one-to-one environment, but what I will touch on does not only occur in a one-to-one environment. The devices are used in a two-tiered dynamic, which furthers the divide. They are only used as a mechanism for intervention—too often from a deficit disposition—or as a reward based upon good performance or good behavior. The intervention not only limits how the device is used, but this intervention is, more often than not, left to be addressed by an application. Consider how efforts around achievement gap mitigation are left to a computer-based platform as the only time a student gets access to a device. Additionally, consider how often students are provided an extrinsic reward for things like work completion or behavior with a "if you do

_____ then you will be allowed to use the computer."

Now let's add artificial intelligence to this whole dynamic. Despite all the efforts and rhetoric around personalization, voice and choice, and my personal favorite, "creativity," within education, none of this can be effectively implemented or addressed unless and until a basic minimum standard is ensured by all. As I have shared, it goes far beyond the distribution of devices. What AI platforms will students have access to? Will they be education-specific platforms? Will the AI functionality be embedded within an existing school ecosystem of applications and programs? Another thing to consider is the quality of platforms in the context of free versus paid versions. While the saying may be old, it never gets old, "When something is free there is a high probability you are the data or product they need." I'd like to add that there is a significant performance and capability difference between many of the free and premium versions of the more popular large language models. All of this is to say, I can imagine a perception that providing access is simply enough, when it is not. I can imagine an attempted remix or implementation of personalization where it is relegated to the AI platform, without any proper vetting of the capabilities or functionality due to reasons we examine in this book. What I want to imagine is the digital divide being at the forefront of all decision making when it comes to the acquisition of and accessibility to digital resources. What I want to imagine, and subsequently see, is AI being an essential resource primarily used to augment a learner's experience, not a luxury provided to a few thus exacerbating the already significant chasm we call the digital divide.

Connecting the Dots: Marginalization, Access, and Classroom AI

Examining the digital landscape in education, we see a complex interplay between marginalization, digital access, and classroom AI. Physical access to devices and connectivity, while crucial, merely scratches the surface. A constellation of social factors orbits the digital divide. Economic disparities cast long shadows over access. More affluent districts hoard state-of-the-art technologies, purchasing the latest devices and fast, reliable connectivity. Meanwhile, economically disadvantaged schools struggle to procure even basic resources. This widens divisions rather than mends them.

Beyond budgets, district policies become architects engineering the contours of access. Restrictive rules that deny access to digital tools inadvertently exclude students from vital learning opportunities. However, thoughtful policies crafted through an equity lens could pave the way to democratized access. Classrooms aren't isolated bubbles; they reflect social inequalities at large. The tech gap is a digital reflection of the wealth gap's gaping chasm. To bridge the divide requires confronting the underlying marginalization that breeds unequal access. Only then can we tap into technology's full potential to empower students across the socioeconomic spectrum.

The digital divide's roots extend deep into our social soil. With concerted effort, we can uplift all learners. But neglecting these roots allows inequities to flourish, which limits technology's capacity to enrich education. It is crucial we see the societal forces shading access to illuminate the path towards equity. As AI-driven education tools proliferate, the gulf between minimal and optimal access profoundly impacts learning. For example, interacting with a basic smartphone chatbot cannot match the educational value and intelligent instruction provided by AI systems purposefully designed for teaching and learning on computer platforms.

Quality differences in devices, connectivity, technical support, and AI model capabilities create a gradient of access. Well-resourced schools implement customized AI tutoring platforms that adapt to students' evolving needs and provide detailed feedback. Under-resourced classrooms may be limited to a glitchy third-party app with canned replies. Network factors also affect access quality. Latency issues from overburdened connections could slow an AI writing assistant to a crawl, while blazing fiber enables seamless generation of ideas, outlines, and drafts. Lack of on-site IT staff to troubleshoot technical problems compounds challenges.

Even with quality devices and networks, lack of accommodations can exclude learners with disabilities and exceptionalities. AI applications must incorporate accessibility best practices such as screen reader compatibility, captioning, and keyboard navigation to equitably serve all students. One-size-fits all AI simply replicates existing disparities. Truly empowering systems must account for diverse interests, backgrounds, and needs. This requires intentional design and concerted efforts to make state-of-the-art AI accessible beyond privileged pockets.

Quality AI access should never be a luxury reserved only for the well-off. Our collective responsibility is to confront systemic gaps and implement solutions that enable all students to benefit from AI's immense learning potential. Equitable access to AI demands looking beyond devices to the experiences enabled. For example, personalized adaptive tutoring platforms allow students to receive customized support and feedback in real-time. There are many platforms that continue to emerge with promises of providing feedback on student writing, time it takes for them to answer questions on multiple choice questions, tracks what students have learned over time and their skill level and even decipher which types of questions and language students struggle with.[20] For a fee, teachers and administrators are provided access to learning analytics dashboards that help them see student responses and suggested interventions.[21] This level of responsive instruction was previously unimaginable. Under-resourced classrooms using only simple chatbots are denied this opportunity for tailored learning.

We have a duty to also examine who holds the power to shape AI development and implementation. Typically, affluent districts design and control their own systems, while poorer ones must accept off-the-shelf products. This imbalance lets those already privileged determine the rules of access. Approaching AI as a dynamic collaboration between educators and technologists can help democratize influence. Teachers and students in underserved communities can provide vital insights to build more responsive tools. Their voices are essential to inoculate against bias and reflect diverse cultures.

Of course, basic adequacy in devices and bandwidth remains crucial. But the bar must extend beyond minimally functioning technology. True equity means empowering the historically excluded and marginalized to become active drivers in advancing quality AI access and realizing its possibilities. This undertaking requires honesty in confronting disparities, then tenacity in advocating for resources and representation. Only when all students can reap AI's benefits, shape its course, and contribute their gifts will the dawn of an inclusive digital learning era be fully realized. The stakes are high, but the potential rewards make our greatest effort imperative.

District policies hold immense power to exacerbate or mitigate divisions in digital access and opportunities. Restrictive policies that outright ban advanced tools or emerging technologies often stem from reactionary concerns. However, this negates students' right to hands-on engagement needed to develop digital literacy and digital fluency. Rather than outright banning emerging technologies like AI, districts can develop guided exploration programs. This allows controlled access for students and teachers to gain both digital literacy and digital fluency while growing a deeper technology acumen. Schools like Marquette High School in Chesterfield, Missouri have taken the risk of enabling students and teachers access to AI tools such ChatGPT and Google Gemini for students to utilize and learn how to utilize effectively.[22]

Monitoring use and collaborating on guidelines empowers rightsholders rather than prohibiting engagement. Careful policy development and protocols for use enables monitoring for equity.[23] We need to ask ourselves: Is AI truly enhancing outcomes for marginalized learners, or is it disproportionately benefiting already privileged students? Regular reassessment guarantees that applications remain aligned with their intended goals, preventing any regression towards bias. With vigilance, wisdom, and human values guiding integration, AI tools can enhance learning equitably. However, it is of the utmost importance that we also acknowledge risks and remain open to course-correcting based on community input. This balancing act requires nuance—neither demonizing nor deifying emerging innovations. If we dismiss AI as too dangerous or celebrate it uncritically, we cede control of its trajectory. Thoughtful development grounded in our shared hopes can steer it towards broad empowerment. But this future must be co-authored with diverse voices, not predetermined in isolation. Our collective hand guides the pen.

Teacher training policies play a pivotal role in shaping the divide. Districts that invest in ongoing professional development empower educators to fluently integrate technology into learning. Conversely, providing inadequate training around digital tools leaves teachers ill-equipped, hindering their full utilization. Top-down directives are not the sole solution. Districts can establish teacher-parent-student councils to offer input and feedback on technology initiatives. This inclusive process empowers diverse rightsholders to help shape policies promoting equitable access.

Policies permeate the foundation of learning, directing resources towards underserved schools, enhancing accessibility, and amplifying marginalized voices. Conversely, they can concentrate opportunities among the privileged. The potential exists to bridge divisions, but only if policies stem from a foundation of social responsibility. The digital divide extends beyond device availability into the essence of learning itself. As we examine its contours, a unifying theme emerges—access is profoundly influenced by social forces.

Economic disparities, policies, training, and inclusive processes all collaborate to widen or narrow the gap. To craft policies that foster equity, we need to step back and analyze the sociological landscape in which access is either expanded or restricted. For technology to equally empower learners, we have an urgent requirement to first empower every voice in the dialogue and address the roots of social inequality that fuel the divide. Only then can we cultivate the fertile ground from which equitable access can flourish.

Promoting Equity: Uneven Access to AI for Creativity and Learning

DL:
By now, it's well established that the pandemic exposed economic disparities between the privileged and the underprivileged—those with abundant resources and those struggling to make ends meet. For schools with wealthier

students and more resources, the pandemic's disruptions were less severe. They didn't face the same challenges as schools scrambling to equip families with Chromebooks and internet access. Students in well-resourced schools, in comparison, already had multiple personal devices, powerful computers, high-speed internet, and premium services for remote learning.

The economic divide became painfully clear when schools mandated cameras on. Some students showcased brightly lit, dedicated study spaces, while others couldn't hide the reality of their homes: kitchens, bedrooms, or younger siblings running around in the background. Some students could blur their backgrounds or create custom scenes using software like Snap Camera, a privilege limited to users with high-end Macs and PCs. These "customizations," meant to address privacy concerns, weren't available for students with the basic hardware provided by schools in the name of equality.

Now, as we emerge from the pandemic, most platforms offer web-based versions originally not designed for education. However, the digital divide persists. It's not just about having the same tools. The real disparity lies in the lack of additional support for students relying on borrowed devices, limited data plans (represented by the green and blue bubbles), and potentially no access to personal tutoring. These students grapple with the same tests, digital worksheets, and essays as their better-equipped peers, all while competing for college admissions and scholarships. The true challenge lies not in simply distributing devices but in acknowledging the existing digital divide and providing tailored support to bridge the gap.

Stark disparities exist between schools in access to advanced AI tools, widening the equity gap instead of closing it. Well-funded districts are in a more favorable position to integrate AI broadly, purchasing premium models to augment instruction and assessment, with teachers receiving extensive training and the resources needed to utilize these tools effectively. Students actively engage in hands-on learning with the technologies. In contrast, under-resourced schools lack the budgets to procure high-level AI tools and platforms with premium safeguards in place, leading to teachers having limited opportunities for direct experience and students having minimal access to develop skills and literacy using the technologies.

This imbalance reflects and exacerbates broader societal inequities, where students able to wield AI as part of their education gain valuable expertise applicable to future careers, while those denied exposure miss out on acquiring technical and creative competencies that could profoundly shape their trajectories. Disparities also arise within districts, as gifted programs and specialized schools concentrate access to emerging technologies among already privileged demographics, compounding inequalities under the guise of "excellence" rather than democratizing opportunity.

Equal access to explore and apply cutting-edge innovations allows students from all backgrounds to see themselves as creators of the future. However, lopsided access promotes the narrative that only certain groups belong on the vanguard of technological progress. AI possesses immense potential to transform learning when thoughtfully implemented; unequal access converts this potential force for educational empowerment into a force for exclusion. Without equity, AI risks becoming a privilege reserved for the few rather than a tool benefiting all.

Those able to harness AI gain exposure to the forefront of innovation. They acquire knowledge and skills transferable to postsecondary studies and career paths. This has become more evident and urgent as AI becomes more and more essential in the context of what seems to be a growing consensus around its impact. In fact, the World Economic Forum estimates that AI will have a significant impact on current as well as future jobs, economies, and help us solve global challenges.[24] However, banning or limiting hands-on engagement with AI for other students slams the door on crucial opportunities. We are compelled to ask ourselves, is it ethical if advancing technology further only advantages those already at the top? Should certain students enjoy access to the most powerful learning tools while others languish in the analog past? Unequal access blatantly contradicts technology's promise as an equalizing force.

Many factors contribute to this equity gap—funding disparities, varying teacher readiness, and expensive proprietary models. However, we have an obligation to also examine the role of internal biases. Do we subconsciously view some students as inherently more deserving of cutting-edge innovations? AI should not entrench privilege, but rather dismantle barriers to access. Closing the equity gap requires acknowledging unfair biases while concurrently addressing tangible resource and training needs. Only through holistic efforts can we realize AI's potential for educational justice.

The time has long since come to mobilize around advocating for equitable access to AI tools and training in our school systems. Turning the tide requires giving voice to hard truths and taking concrete steps. We are required to first openly acknowledge how unchecked biases allow gaps in access to persist and proliferate. Historical marginalization cannot be used as justification to deny anyone opportunities to shape the future. As previously stated, district leaders play a pivotal role through funding allocations, policies, and messaging. However, citizens also bear responsibility. We can collectively demand that officials prioritize equitable distribution of emerging technologies and related teacher professional development. The status quo of unequal access to AI is unacceptable. It will take our collective work together—educators, parents, students, and community organizations—to dismantle these barriers. By acknowledging systemic injustices, taking action through targeted programs, and sustaining our efforts, we can unlock the true potential of AI to uplift all communities.

Tools for Equity: Making Educational AI More Equitably Accessible

Bridging pervasive divides in access to AI demands comprehensive initiatives across multiple dimensions. While funding is crucial, money alone cannot overcome systemic gaps without accompanying efforts to make emerging technologies inclusive and educators AI-fluent. Public funding must be allocated equitably, prioritizing procurement of advanced AI tools for schools with the greatest needs. However, free accessibility should also be expanded, such as through models adapted specifically for education and open courseware to build teacher capabilities.

To create AI tutors that empower all learners, we need to consider inclusive design features from the very beginning. Instead of merely providing answers, AI tutors should offer step-by-step explanations of their reasoning process. This transparency promotes deeper understanding and allows for learner agency in their decision-making. Additionally, providing options like text input, voice commands, or touch-based interfaces empowers students with diverse needs and preferences. Using clear and concise instructions throughout the interface avoids technical jargon, making the AI tutor accessible and inviting for all students. For example, many AI tools can already be asked to provide a rationale for their responses. This allows learners to understand the logic behind those responses, giving them the agency to make informed decisions based on AI recommendations. By following these principles, AI tutors can become a powerful tool for personalized learning, benefiting a wider range of students and unlocking their full potential.

Grassroots community partnerships offer powerful pathways for bridging the digital divide and giving students firsthand experience with AI. By collaborating with museums and libraries, schools can tap into existing resources like AI exhibits or workshops that introduce core concepts in engaging ways. Partnerships with local tech companies can open doors to guest speakers, mentorships, and even access to cutting-edge AI tools unavailable within the classroom. For example, by partnering with existing STEM centers, such as The Engineer Factory STEM Center in Los Angeles, California[25] and Do Greater in Charlotte, North Carolina,[26] grassroots organizations can leverage existing infrastructure and expertise to develop impactful AI programs. After-school programs focused on STEM provide an ideal setting for hands-on learning with AI through interactive games or coding activities. Designed specifically for Black and Brown youth and their parents, these programs would integrate AI skills training, ethical discussions, and hands-on engagement with technology. This collaborative approach maximizes resources and fosters a more equitable AI landscape, empowering marginalized communities to actively shape the technological revolution. These community partnerships broaden access and exposure, sparking interest and building confidence. Through inclusive AI tool design and proactive community outreach, we can ensure that every student, regardless of background, has the opportunity to engage with and benefit from the transformative power of AI.

Teacher readiness also plays a crucial role in ensuring that AI is used equitably within the classroom. Ongoing professional development opportunities can empower educators with the knowledge and skills they need to leverage AI responsibly, while avoiding any unintentional exacerbation of existing disparities. Workshops focused on bias mitigation, ethical use cases, and inclusive teaching strategies provide essential training. By raising awareness of how bias can manifest in AI and offering concrete strategies for mitigating it, these workshops help teachers make informed decisions about AI tools. Similarly, exploring ethical use case scenarios helps teachers understand the broader implications of AI and develop a critical lens for its use. Finally, training in how to integrate AI into inclusive lesson plans supports a more equitable learning experience for all students. Supplementing this formal training with opportunities for peer collaboration allows teachers to share best practices, learn from each other, and build a collective sense of responsibility for the responsible use of AI in classrooms.

As AI rapidly evolves, one-time training quickly becomes obsolete. Teachers and students require ongoing learning opportunities to stay literate with AI advancements. Sustained professional development enables educators to continually expand their competencies in applying AI for instruction, assessment, and inclusion. Hands-on workshops, virtual seminars, and interactive online resources help teachers keep pace with innovation. To prepare students for a world increasingly shaped by AI, we have a duty to empower them as critical thinkers who understand the societal implications of this technology. Courses specifically designed to explore AI ethics, embedded biases, and the broader consequences for society provide a crucial foundation. However, knowledge alone is not enough. By asking students to actively identify real-world problems where AI may be a solution, while also considering potential pitfalls, we position them as change agents capable of co-designing better solutions. Peer-to-peer learning programs offer unique benefits. Students who grasp AI concepts can lead workshops for their peers, fostering leadership skills and democratizing knowledge more widely. The act of teaching others reinforces their own understanding and cultivates a sense of community dedicated to learning.

Empowering students to think critically about AI's societal impact can be fostered through engaging project-based learning. For instance, students could delve into a news story about how bias affects facial recognition algorithms, discussing the potential consequences and brainstorming how the technology could be redesigned to be more equitable. Similarly, students could identify a local community problem, such as food insecurity, directly aligning with the Sustainable Development Goal of Zero Hunger.[27] They could then research whether and how AI-powered solutions might optimize food distribution systems, address food waste reduction, or predict and manage crop yields in a sustainable manner. To promote peer-to-peer learning, schools could establish after-school "AI clubs." Within these clubs, students with a stronger grasp of AI concepts could prepare and lead mini-lessons for their peers and teachers, covering fundamental concepts and real-world applications.

At all levels, learners should see themselves reflected in AI's evolution. Curriculum and activities showcasing contributions from underrepresented groups provides inspirational mirrors. This helps rectify the lack of diversity plaguing many tech fields. With holistic preparation, this generation can steer AI based on lived realities. Their voices are essential to crafting technology that emancipates rather than oppresses. In fact, there is a quote from Dr. Alondra Nelson that is applicable in this context, "If we want to understand anything about science and technology, we need to begin with the people who have been most damaged, the most subjugated by it. "[28] With concerted efforts across these multilayered avenues, transformative technologies can shift from being exclusive advantages for the privileged few into empowering gateways that unlock potential for all learners regardless of circumstances. This holistic approach that combines funding, accessibility, training, partnerships, and inclusion helps pave the way for AI to make real equity inroads.

Promoting problem-solving skills and a willingness to experiment with emerging technologies in the classroom empowers students to become adaptable lifelong learners. By encouraging young people to see themselves as explorers, they can gain vital skills and understanding. Rotating access to new AI models and collaborating to discover how they work can spark curiosity. It's also essential to create space for examining the societal impacts and potential biases present in AI systems.

Furthermore, partnerships with universities can provide access to cutting-edge research and tools that may not be widely available. Student teaching programs create opportunities for supervised classroom experimentation with new models. Relationships with tech firms could unlock access to tailored AI solutions, with engineers collaborating with educators to design inclusive classroom apps that meet specialized learning needs. Mentoring programs led by machine learning engineers, data scientists, and AI researchers can give students real-world exposure to development practices. It's important to note that some current AI-related roles may become less relevant over time, such as prompt engineering, while new roles will emerge as the technology advances. Encouraging Black and Brown students to develop interest and skills in AI today is essential in building a more equitable future.

Cooperating with nonprofits builds capacity for social change. Joint initiatives could apply AI to address community problems like health disparities or climate justice. Partnering with nonprofits like Generation180 deepens the impact of social reform by engaging students in creative solutions.[29] Generation180's Climate Comedy Cohort, for instance, uses humor to educate about clean energy, while their Storytelling program empowers students to share narratives that inspire action. AI can further amplify these efforts. Students can use AI tools to analyze data on local energy use, informing school initiatives like those championed by Generation180. This practical application fosters understanding of both local sustainability challenges and ethical AI practices. Publicly sharing these collaborative efforts, which could involve student-created climate comedy videos or AI-powered infographics, raises awareness and fosters a culture of ongoing education and innovation.

Beyond one-off projects, sustaining these relationships over time fosters fluency. Regular feedback loops enable evolving tools responsive to classroom realities. Through ongoing dialogue, research and practice continually realign. With strong bridges to research and industry, classrooms stay attuned to AI's pulse. Most vitally, collaboration embeds schools within wider ecosystems that are advancing innovation for the common good. Keeping knowledge current amidst AI's perpetual motion demands ongoing pursuit of learning for all involved. Consistent exposure, dedicated training mechanisms, hands-on exploration, and diverse partnerships provide valuable touchpoints for students, teachers, and communities to sustain engagement with emerging possibilities. Realizing AI's potential while mitigating risks requires instilling skills for responsible and ethical application. Teacher training should incorporate critical perspectives to uncover potential biases as well as developing AI literacy. Structured ethics modules can spur reflection on balancing benefits and drawbacks of algorithmic systems.

In classrooms, scaffolding activities guide students through applying AI incrementally, as a complement to human intelligence. Initial projects may focus on using AI for research and creative inspiration. Later, students analyze use cases and tradeoffs through structured debates and reflect on the implications. This builds capacity and agency in wielding these powerful tools. Multidisciplinary, collaborative projects catalyze ingenuity in AI use while underscoring ethical implications. Learners could jointly create AI-based art installations reflecting on digital culture or build interactive maps showcasing community heritage and knowledge. These initiatives reinforce the reality that technology is a human creation to make a positive difference.

A culture of open, non-judgmental dialogue creates space for questioning and **transparency in AI**'s evolution. Students and teachers should feel empowered to continuously re-examine purposes, evaluate outcomes, and make constructive adjustments in integration. Accepting AI systems as perpetually unfinished drafts permits more conscientious, ethical co-design. Guiding learners to see themselves as responsible authors shaping AI instills agency and care. Immersive experiences as creators, critics and ethicists build essential understanding. With informed engagement, wisdom, empathy and collective responsibility, we can help write AI's future as a story of empowerment for all.

As digital tools evolve at breakneck speeds, the risk of exacerbating existing inequities looms ominously. However, embracing this moment as an inflection point allows us to chart a new course towards justice and empowerment. With intention, wisdom and solidarity, we can co-author a future where emerging technologies unlock human potential rather than constrain it. The current focus on engaging students of color and girls through coding education is a valuable starting point. However, it is essential that we build on this foundation by expanding access and literacy specifically for AI technologies. Rather than presenting basic coding skills as the ceiling, we need to elevate AI proficiency as an important new horizon for empowerment.

With thoughtful framing, AI training can celebrate the unique cultural knowledge and lived experiences students of color and girls bring to understanding and shaping technology. Programs grounded in community heritage that reclaim diverse narratives have rich potential. Positioning AI competence not just as a pathway out of disadvantage but as a way to uplift communities can inspire students to become leaders and change agents steering the future of AI. Making state-of-the-art education and real-world training in applied AI accessible reframes tech literacy. It elevates underrepresented youth as architects of progress capable of addressing local needs and advancing equity. But this requires dedicated efforts to move beyond introductory coding to actively facilitating mastery of transformative AI systems and skills.

AI education grounded in community heritage re-centers marginalized voices. Students can develop tools preserving neighborhood stories, promoting equity, or addressing local challenges. This fosters agency and self-efficacy. Partnerships with minority-led organizations bring vital perspectives on needs. Our perspective must encompass more than just coding skills. Media literacy, ethics, sociology, and history provide contextual knowledge to evaluate AI systems. Multidisciplinary projects build connection, creativity and critical thinking. The humanities balance technical skills with inclusive values.

Rather than assimilationist models, education can nurture **pluralism**. Students should feel welcomed to bring their full identities and experiences to shape technology's arc. AI coded by diverse hands has immense potential for humanity. This vision summons our courage to confront injustice and plant seeds of possibility. When we nourish and celebrate pluralism, fields of innovation can blossom in wondrous diversity. The future unfurls when all of us help cultivate it, stretching toward the sun. There will always be more to discuss and new insights to integrate. If we till the soil for equity, sow ideas broadly, and nourish growth everywhere, the fruits of our labor can feed future generations. Together, we can write a new chapter, where innovation sings in all voices, AI mimics the neural diversity of its makers, and technologies finally reflect the glorious plurality they were destined to empower.

CHAPTER 4

AI and High-Stakes Decisions in Schools

Careful Considerations: Admissions, Grading, Tracking

The educational discourse surrounding AI often espouses an optimistic vision brimming with promises of enhanced efficiency, personalized learning, and data-driven objectivity. However, this rosy narrative warrants careful interrogation. What frequently lurks below the surface are critical considerations and potential perils hidden within prevailing assumptions—the subtle, sometimes intentionally, overlooked areas and equity detours that can derail technological solutions.

To illustrate this point, consider the current enthusiasm for AI-powered social-emotional learning robots, such as ABii[30] and Moxie.[31] These robots are equipped with cameras and sensors designed to decipher students' emotions as they engage in school tasks. They intervene by redirecting attention if students become distracted, offering comfort if they appear despondent, and providing motivation during challenging activities. While the intention of supporting student well-being through technology appears commendable, it prompts a vital question: Have we thoroughly examined the deeper ramifications?

How reliable is emotional interpretation across diverse cultural backgrounds? What biases might be embedded in the AI algorithms, shaping how behaviors are flagged as problematic? The boundary between supportive mechanisms and intrusive surveillance blurs when students are constantly monitored through facial expression analysis and nonverbal cues.

Further, the anthropomorphic design of these robots, often depicted as white, is troubling. Research suggests black robots may be perceived as more threatening, perpetuating harmful stereotypes.[32] Before widely implementing AI-driven social-emotional learning tools, it is crucial to the point of urgency, we demand rigorous ethical frameworks, transparency, and a critical examination of potential biases.

A thorough examination of these issues is crucial if we are to avoid the unintended consequences that often accompany rapid technological advancement. We are obligated to move beyond the allure of efficiency and personalization to illuminate the broader societal landscape that shapes how AI systems are constructed, deployed, and experienced. Scrutinizing underlying assumptions, challenging the aura of neutrality, and centering issues of transparency and accountability are essential for building an ethical foundation for AI—one that elevates diversity, equity, and the irreplaceable human element in education.

The challenge is compounded by the multifaceted nature of AI, from sophisticated **neural networks** to chatbot interfaces.

When assessing high-stakes applications like admissions, grading, and student tracking, a nuanced understanding of different technologies is crucial. Furthermore, we are duty-bound to interrogate the intentions and incentives driving AI adoption, particularly among administrators. While optimized outputs, predictable trajectories, and tightly calibrated processes may serve administrative interests, they risk dehumanizing the educational journey.

This critical conversation forms the bedrock for confronting the complex ways automation and equity intertwine. We have a pressing need to approach AI in education with both clear-sightedness and a commitment to human values. Only by grappling with the profound implications of high-stakes AI can we shape a future where technology serves as a tool, guided by ethical principles. This path demands that we ask difficult questions, but with courage, we can chart a course towards genuine progress. A crucial test case lies in the admissions process, from K-12 private schools to elite universities. These gateways have long been shaped by historical exclusion, with Black, Brown, and Native American students disproportionately facing systemic barriers.[33] Data used by AI systems often reflects this legacy of discrimination. Uncritical reliance on AI threatens to solidify these injustices under the guise of technological neutrality.

Consider the intricate choreography of the human application review of college admittance applications, as exemplified by university admissions committees. Multiple readers meticulously analyze factors like academic coursework, course rigor, special circumstances, extracurriculars, school profiles, and essays, attempting to reconstruct the messy complexities of each applicant's reality. This empathetic sleuthing unveils hidden potential and talent that sterile statistics cannot capture.

KS:

From 2003 to 2010 I was an application reader for my alma mater UCLA (Go Bruins!). This endeavor was a revealing experience in regard to how extensive the process is for vetting both freshman and transfer applications. A significant and essential component of the review process is every single application was reviewed by at least three completely different readers prior to an additional review by the University Admissions and Relations with Schools (UARS) staff. Many of the metrics reviewed are much more objective when you consider things like weighted and unweighted grade point average, test scores, and pretty much anything that had a definitive numerical value attached to it. Where the nuance and "human element" becomes essential to this process are things like reading the essays, looking at extracurriculars, and applying all of these metrics along with the school profile to assign a score. Note: Readers never make any final decisions; they score applications and sometimes provide recommendations for additional review mechanisms. A significant and essential part of this process that can never, and should never, be replaced by an algorithm is the process of looking at the application in its entirety, while also considering the context of the essay, profile of the school, availability of higher rigorous academic courses, accessibility to critical learning resources, and several additional factors only a human can assess. Here is an example, applicant A attends a well-resourced school that offers a plethora of honors and advanced placement classes. The school has a robust athletics program, performing arts department, and a wide range of on campus activities that can not only bolster an application, but also provide a window into how that student contributes to the greater campus community. Applicant B attends a school that either lacks the resources or the ability to hire and retain staff that is certified to teach advanced placement courses. In comparison, the applicant has taken only three of these types of courses whereas applicant A has taken more than a dozen. Due to homelife circumstances as well, applicant B has to work part time during the school year and full time during the summer. Their opportunities to engage in extracurricular activities are severely impacted by a lack of availability in their schedule. Let's add that both applicants have shown a consistently high performance in their classes as indicated by their weighted and unweighted GPA. They both explain in their personal statements how their experiences shape their commitment to learning, personal growth, and dreams for the future. Let's add that applicant B is also a first-generation college applicant. When you apply these within a historical context, an algorithm is likely to prioritize the accomplishments of applicant A due to the over-emphasis and hyper value placed on grade point average, standardized test scores, and likely, campus activity participation. None of the above should be, nor can be responsibly, left to automation via an algorithm. This can, and likely will, become an even greater concern should AI become a part of this process as examined below.

But what happens when this dance between human reviewers is replaced by algorithmic analysis? Trained on historical data saturated with inequalities, AI systems inherit deeply rooted biases. Students from disadvantaged backgrounds face implicit penalties on inputs like access to advanced courses and enrichment activities outside their control. Rather than dismantling barriers, high-stakes admissions AI could build higher walls, amplifying existing disparities through code rather than prejudice.

At the crux of this dilemma looms the question of whether high-stakes decisions with lasting impacts on young lives, like college admissions, should ultimately rest in robotic hands. Is there no room left for human discernment and empathy in recognizing latent talent and potential, regardless of background? As the gates of opportunity swing open or closed, it becomes a matter of necessity that we carefully weigh the risks of ceding to algorithms the human art of perceiving promise amidst the shadows.

Beyond admissions, high-stakes decisions around grading and assessment present another complex domain for AI integration, demanding thoughtful examination. When statistical algorithms replace human evaluators, the richness of subjective academic judgment gets stripped away in the quest for standardized data points. But can this truly foster robust learning, creativity and potential? The origins of the data consumed by grading algorithms warrants scrutiny. Metrics like standardized test scores, often touted as "objective," frequently reflect institutional biases rather than comprehensive snapshots of developing minds. Training AI on such data risks propagating historical discrimination rather than dismantling it.

Research suggests a growing recognition of the limited correlation between high-stakes test performance and long-term student success. We encourage you to investigate this further by attempting the following prompt in two or more LLMs:

Fact-check the following statement: Numerous studies and research findings have indicated a growing recognition of the limited correlation between high-stakes test performance and long-term student success. Cite your sources. Once the LLM reveals its results, your next task is to authenticate the sources and the validity of the sources.

What did you learn? This insight challenges the traditional belief that high scores on standardized tests directly translate to sustained academic achievement and overall success in students' educational journeys. Through various research endeavors, scholars have shed light on the complex and multifaceted nature of student success, emphasizing the need to consider diverse factors beyond test outcomes when evaluating and predicting long-term educational outcomes. Yet policies and funding remain tied to these reductive barometers, due to entrenched financial and political interests. This magnifies the danger of entrusting AI grading systems with outsized influence over academic fates based on questionable notions of "merit." At its core, high-stakes assessment involves complex social philosophies and goals. But unfettered enthusiasm for data-driven grading risks reducing rich academic inquiry to sterilized quantifiable metrics. Because of this we have a pressing need to carefully examine the human values and educational aims underpinning assessment before further ceding authority to AI.

The use of AI in tracking and categorizing students also warrants critical analysis, as labels carry lasting impacts. Often under the banner of "data-driven" reform, schools embrace narrow definitions of success, such as performance in specific topics like math and reading. Students get branded through this reductive lens, ignoring their multifaceted talents. Well-intentioned interventions inspired by such metrics, like test-prep drills, frequently lack research grounding and deepen inequities. Arts, sports and humanities suffer budget cuts to double down on the tested subjects that determine rankings. This commodification of learning erodes holistic development in favor of chasing standardized scores.

Research on bias in educational data, such as standardized testing, has revealed significant racial and socioeconomic disparities that disadvantage certain student groups.[34] This inherent bias within the data itself creates a dangerous situation: training predictive AI on such data risks perpetuating these historical injustices.[35] As the saying goes, "garbage in, garbage out"—biased data leads to biased algorithms that reinforce existing inequalities rather than empower the diverse talents of all students.

A truly transformative shift requires us to move beyond simply scrutinizing the data we use. It is paramount that we fundamentally rethink the very goals that determine how students are categorized and tracked. These goals have often been based on narrow metrics that fail to capture the holistic potential of each child. Instead, we need to build learning ecosystems that celebrate individuality and nurture the unique potential within every student. Only then can AI ethically support a truly equitable educational landscape, where technology serves as a tool to empower all learners, celebrating their unique strengths and contributions, not perpetuating past injustices.

Propagating Partiality: AI's Potential to Perpetuate Injustice

When developing AI systems for high-stakes educational decisions, rigorous scrutiny of the training data is crucial. Historical datasets are often riddled with societal biases, and their uncritical use can lead to algorithms that perpetuate, or even amplify, existing injustices.[36] Legacy biases around race, gender, **socioeconomic status**, and disability status persist in outdated statistics, academic records, and test results. Training AI admissions algorithms on such data, for example, would inevitably replicate historical inequities, denying opportunities to marginalized groups.[37]

Attempts to achieve neutrality through "colorblind" AI, which ignores sensitive attributes like race and ethnicity, are misguided. Systemic biases extend far beyond easily identifiable demographic factors. This approach disregards the complex ways in which societal inequities are reflected in seemingly neutral data.[38] Striving for neutrality without prioritizing equity is akin to the California Civil Rights Initiative of 1996 (Proposition 209), which outlawed affirmative action programs in public institutions. While Proposition 209 aimed to achieve a race-neutral playing field, critics argued it masked underlying biases that continued to disadvantage certain minority groups.[39] Similarly, seeking proxy inputs—seemingly neutral factors correlated with race or other protected attributes—is ethically risky. This practice, like Proposition 209's predictable consequences, risks creating new forms of discrimination, perpetuating injustices through seemingly objective algorithms. Blindly relying on historical data, riddled with societal prejudices, is not a solution. We have no choice but to move beyond a facade of neutrality and actively work towards equitable AI in education.

The development of fair and inclusive AI in education demands a shift away from blindly feeding algorithms historical data. It is paramount that we adopt a critical approach and proactively work against potential biases. **Data weighting** is one vital tool. It works like a seesaw, where we adjust the weights on each side to find balance. If the training data overrepresents students from affluent backgrounds, data weighting allows us to give more importance to data points from underrepresented groups, thus minimizing the system's tendency to favor certain groups over others. Another tool to combat inaccurate, incomplete, or irrelevant data within the datasets would be **data cleansing**. This process not only removes problematic data but also is another tactic for mitigating bias. It does, however, come with a minor caveat. Unless the data cleansing has safeguards in place and is thoughtfully implemented, it runs a very real risk of recreating the bias it potentially removes, thus perpetuating the very thing it is supposed to address.

In addition to data weighting and data cleansing, **algorithmic auditing** and external oversight by experts are crucial tools for identifying and correcting biases. Companies at the forefront of ethical AI development, like Latimer.ai, emphasize this approach. Auditing helps to reveal historical biases embedded in the AI system, while external oversight ensures ethical considerations remain central. Continuous tuning is another essential practice. AI systems aren't static; therefore, it requires us to continuously monitor and adjust them to adapt to new information and avoid solidifying biases over time. These proactive measures are vital if we intend to use AI to empower all students, not reinforce past injustices. Only by honestly confronting historical biases within data can we create a truly equitable educational landscape where technology serves as a force for good.

One significant hazard arising from the increasing utilization of algorithms within education systems is the prevalent misconception of neutrality. It is erroneous to assume that AI systems are inherently "unbiased" simply because they may overlook sensitive attributes like race or gender. This form of decontextualized neutrality does not guarantee fairness. Instead, it obscures the impact of social structures and historical patterns on individual student experiences.[40] For instance, consider an admissions AI that professes objectivity by disregarding race but then bases decisions on seemingly neutral proxies such as school quality and extracurricular activities. These proxies are significantly influenced by historical exclusion and ongoing resource disparities. Insisting on artificial neutrality diverts attention from the crucial task of actively combating systemic biases, while also undermining the documented advantages of diverse learning environments. Studies have demonstrated that exposure to varied backgrounds and perspectives cultivates critical thinking skills, creativity, and cultural awareness in students. Prioritizing neutrality over inclusive representation perpetuates the status quo and hinders meaningful progress towards achieving equity.

Rather than pursuing an illusion, we have to diligently and carefully contextualize the data fed into AI systems. This entails integrating insights from the social sciences and humanities into the design process.[41] Solely focusing on numbers and statistics will inadequately capture the intricate educational obstacles faced by marginalized students. Emphasizing equitable outcomes over the illusion of neutrality is paramount. This process will necessitate addressing deep-rooted inequalities, a challenging yet indispensable endeavor. To ensure that AI fosters justice in education instead of perpetuating historical injustices, we are ethically bound to bravely confront these uncomfortable truths.

Myopic enthusiasm for artificial intelligence risks glossing over its potential to silently amplify exclusion and inequity if applied negligently in education. A closer examination reveals myriad ways unchecked AI could in fact stall progress, from admissions algorithms encoding generational discrimination, to biased personalized tutors failing marginalized students, to chatbots unconsciously absorbing harmful tropes. For example, predictive models trained solely to maximize schoolwide test scores could steer resources disproportionately towards students near passing thresholds at the expense of minoritized peers. Admissions systems claiming an empty neutrality by ignoring race may still perpetuate bias through facially neutral inputs like access to advanced courses and extracurriculars shaped by past and present systemic barriers. Lack of diversity in AI design risks that tools will fail to meet all students' needs.

These cautionary examples underscore the need for continuous critical vigilance, multidisciplinary oversight, and centering marginalized voices when building education AI systems. Without such conscientious scrutiny, the door opens dangerously wide for technology to silently amplify prejudice rather than unlock potential. As stewards of progress, it is vital that we illuminate shadowy areas, call out risks of tokenization, and demand that emerging innovations walk the walk of equity, or they have no place in our schools. With care, AI can counter disadvantage; without care, it will only compound injustice.

Transparent and Accountable: Fostering Trust Through Disclosure

DL:

Here's a fun activity I enjoy asking workshop participants to engage in: try asking multiple AI tools questions about a topic you know a lot about. This will help you understand how different tools work, how accurately they represent information, and their comparative strengths and weaknesses. Most importantly, this exercise reveals how forthcoming the tools are about where they source their information and how they process it.

To illustrate this, I remind you all that I began my teaching career teaching business. I would have my students do a Google search on their names to promote awareness of credit scores and online identity management. We would then work on building their online portfolios to improve their profiles. In the same spirit, if you have a strong online presence, I recommend asking several AI tools, "Who is [insert your name]?"

At the time of the writing of this book, I attempted this exercise for myself by asking "Who is Dee Lanier" on free versions of Microsoft Copilot, Perplexity AI, Latimer, Claude, and Google Gemini. The results were surprisingly inconsistent. Microsoft Copilot and Perplexity AI both provided detailed, accurate responses with citations clearly pulled from the internet. Latimer gave correct information but didn't include citations. Claude simply stated it lacked information about me, and Google Gemini claimed the same, despite Google search easily retrieving relevant information. Further, Gemini accurately summarizes and cites my published works, so its inability to locate biographical data is puzzling.

While Claude and Gemini are both excellent tools for other purposes, their lack of transparency regarding how they source and utilize data from the web raises concerns about their effectiveness for research. Without understanding their selection process, it's difficult to assess the comprehensiveness and accuracy of the information they provide. This opacity across platforms hinders users' ability to make informed decisions about the trustworthiness of the information they receive.

Realizing the responsible promise of AI in education necessitates transparency. Understanding how these technologies are built and how they make decisions is imperative. Students, parents, educators and communities have a right to know the inner workings of algorithms that carry high stakes for academic futures. At the foundation, transparency is required in the training data used to develop education AI systems. The size and diversity of datasets determine an algorithm's real-world applicability. Without representative data, flaws propagate. Disclosure enables scrutiny.

Additionally, the selection and processing of input features used must be open to inspection. Choices in how algorithms are constructed shape outputs. Transparency empowers users to ask important questions, like whether inputs reflect equitable considerations or perpetuate disadvantage. Finally, accountability mechanisms must exist when AI falls short of ethical aims. Freedom of information laws should encompass automated decision systems. Like human governance, code-based governance requires checks and balances to remedy errors and harms. Only through transparency can we achieve algorithmic accountability and uphold ethics.

While AI promises invaluable insights, retaining meaningful human oversight remains essential for ethical application in high-stakes educational decisions. Human reviewers provide nuanced context beyond even the most sophisticated algorithms. It is important to note that there is no perfect solution here. Human reviewers are still likely to render evaluations and decisions within the domain of their own biases, but this is much more likely to be addressed than learning it through automation. In domains like admissions, multiple human readers allow holistic assessment, weighing factors like adversity overcome and listening for silenced voices. AI can enhance by flagging potential biases, but humans must audit outputs to catch subtle exclusions.

For consequential decisions like tracking into advanced or remedial paths, AI informed human discernment is imperative. Beyond performance data, human guidance advisors incorporate motivations, challenges and goals. Multifaceted success cannot be reduced to numbers. Humans must be empowered to override flawed AI. Grading algorithms demanding rigid rubrics may miss unconventional creative brilliance. Human moderation preserves space for inspired innovation, not just programmed outputs.

At its core, education involves complex social values beyond computation—empathy, ethics, intellectual courage. Humans must oversee AI to uphold these ideals and prevent data-driven determinism. With vigilance, technology can augment without erasing humanistic education. Truly embedding ethical artificial intelligence into the fabric of high-stakes educational decisions will require establishing new mechanisms of governance and community-centered oversight. It is essential we move beyond lofty principles into actively encoding transparency, accountability and human primacy into the design, deployment and regulation of learning algorithms.

While AI offers extraordinary potential to personalize learning and streamline educational processes, its use demands careful consideration. Code alone cannot ensure fairness and prevent unintended harm. To achieve equitable AI in education, it is of the utmost importance that we establish a robust sociotechnical ecosystem driven by several core principles. Regional authorities must mandate comprehensive algorithmic impact assessments before any AI system with the potential to significantly impact students' academic trajectories is deployed.[42] These assessments will analyze potential biases, disparate outcomes, and broader societal impacts. Families, educators, technology experts, and students themselves must be empowered as rightsholders, playing active roles in the participatory design of AI tools to ensure these systems reflect their needs and values.[43]

Federal agencies must proactively develop clear frameworks prohibiting algorithmic discrimination in education, encompassing both technical standards for fairness and addressing broader social impacts.[44] For publicly funded AI innovations, transparency is essential, with key information like training datasets, error audits, and bias mitigation strategies made publicly accessible.[45] Finally, whistleblowers must be protected by dedicated channels, shielding them from retaliation and ensuring ethical concerns are promptly addressed.[46] This ecosystem is about maximizing the potential of AI to uplift all learners. By proactively merging legal guidelines, institutional responsibility, and the collective wisdom of our communities, we can harness AI as a tool for progress guided by our shared commitment to equity and justice in education.

Of course, technical fluency among educators, families and learners themselves provides a vital check on unethical deployments. We therefore have a responsibility to cultivate AI literacy and awareness at all levels of society. Only through multifaceted governance that merges ethics, education, law, and community wisdom can AI systems be held to account. The story we write through today's choices shapes tomorrow's realities. We have a responsibility to take up the pen of progress through strategic governance that charges technology with serving students, not systems.

CHAPTER 5

Synthetic Media in the Classroom

Creating Counterfeits: Fake Audio, Images, and Video

DL:

I'm a hip-hop enthusiast. Remember back in 2012 when the internet exploded over the Tupac hologram at Coachella? It was mind-blowing—a technological wonder, but also a little eerie. It wasn't just seeing an iconic rapper back on stage, but the way it recreated his mannerisms and tattoos, fueling old rumors that he might still be alive. He even shouted, "What the f--- is up, Coachellaaaaa!" Could this really be him? That performance gave us a glimpse into the future of AI. Now, imagine what took months of work back then and could be done in a fraction of the time with proper prompt engineering. AI can generate turn-by-turn directions in a celebrity's voice, release "new" music, even create stand-up routines. It raises ethical questions about using the voices and images of those who have passed away. But the issue gets even thornier with living artists. We'll get back to that, for the record.

Synthetic media. The very phrase conjures images of deepfakes, of digital replicas blurring the lines between truth and fiction. In this chapter, we explore this phenomenon, not just within the confines of the classroom, but with ramifications far beyond academic walls. While some, perhaps rightfully, raise concerns about plagiarism and copyright infringement, it also goes much deeper than that. Consider hip-hop, where sampling—borrowing snippets from existing music and reworking them—is a foundational element of the genre. Across all styles, musicians frequently integrate melodies, lyrics, and rhythms into their original work. However, the advent of AI blurs the distinction between homage and appropriation.

In April 2023, the rap group AllttA released an unnerving AI-generated collaboration with Jay-Z, raising questions about artistic integrity. This event sparked debates in schools and universities worldwide, questioning whether such creations are innovative or constitute intellectual theft. This controversy echoes the then-ongoing rap beef between heavyweights Drake and Kendrick Lamar. In hip-hop, these "beefs" are a competitive tradition of diss tracks exchanged between artists. Yet, as fans eagerly awaited each artist's response, AI introduced a new element: doubt about the authenticity of the songs. AI's ability to mimic voices made it difficult to discern whether the music was genuinely from one's favorite artist. This is a defining characteristic of our current era.

Even more concerning is how synthetic media could manipulate elections or criminal investigations. How can we trust anything online when "fake news" is routinely dismissed, and AI-generated content creates a landscape of plausible deniability? Let's move beyond the theoretical and consider how voice manipulation directly impacts our personal lives and livelihoods. Voice training began with services like Goog-411 (that's back in the day for those that remember) and continues with assistants like Alexa, Siri, and Google Assistant. If rap artists can have their voices used without consent in realistic new releases, how concerned should we be about our data being weaponized against us? Imagine police interrogation tactics where they manipulate facts to force a confession, claiming "we have you on tape" and playing back a falsified recording.

When AI-powered language models such as ChatGPT first surfaced, the primary alarms rang over fears of copyright infringement. Authors and artists lamented, "How can we safeguard intellectual property?" Likewise, educators started to inquire, "How can we deter students from committing plagiarism?" As creatives, we echo these concerns. While the conversation around AI focuses on copyright theft and false credit, Black and Brown people in the US face a deeper fear. Synthetic media terrifies us with its potential to be weaponized for false accusations and wrongful imprisonment.

Consider the chilling case of Robert Williams, wrongfully arrested in 2020 based on flawed **facial recognition technology**.[47] His story is a stark reminder that the dangers of synthetic media extend far beyond viral entertainment. Here, the victim wasn't a celebrity caught in a media crossfire; it was an ordinary man thrust into the nightmarish maze of a false accusation; his identity stolen by lines of code. Robert Williams, a father of two, was apprehended in front of his horrified family based on a faulty match from a grainy security camera image. He spent 30 hours in jail, his reputation tarnished, his life upended by an algorithm's mistake. This incident, documented by the ACLU, shows the terrifying potential for synthetic media to become a tool for racial profiling and wrongful accusations, particularly against vulnerable communities.

Unlike deepfakes of celebrities, which are often humorous or attention-grabbing, misused facial recognition can have devastating real-world consequences. The risk extends beyond law enforcement to educational settings, where AI detectors aimed at preventing cheating can lead to false accusations. This over-policing contributes to the school-to-prison pipeline. Whether perpetrated by school resource officers or local police, technical errors that lead to false accusations erode trust, traumatize innocent people, and exacerbate racial biases within the justice system. The Robert Williams case serves as a cautionary tale, urging us to be wary of deploying technologies that prioritize convenience over accuracy, especially when those inaccuracies disproportionately impact Black and Brown people.

As Michelle Alexander writes in her book, *The New Jim Crow*, "The widespread use of surveillance technology, such as license plate readers, facial recognition software, and predictive policing algorithms, has allowed the criminal justice system to monitor, track, and target people of color in unprecedented ways."[48] We see not just stolen words and melodies, but lives potentially uprooted, reputations shattered on the altar of synthetic fabrication. Could a student's voice be mimicked to create a false confession of a crime he didn't commit? Could a carefully crafted video twist someone's words beyond recognition? The prospect of synthetic media being misused to frame Black and Brown students terrifies us.

This, you see, is the chilling potential of synthetic media. It's not just about stolen verses or misattributed melodies. It's about the weaponization of truth, the ability to manufacture reality with terrifying precision. This is why media literacy must transcend rote antiquated lessons on plagiarism and copyright laws. It must become a shield against manipulation masquerading as progress. We have to equip our teachers and administrators with the latest tools to dissect, analyze, and question the very pixels on their screens. Imagine workshops that train them to identify deepfakes and uncover the fingerprints of manipulation hidden within seemingly innocuous videos. Furthermore, we have a moral obligation to equip students and parents on how to have **"the talk"** as it relates to AI and deepfakes.

While the legal and ethical implications of synthetic media, particularly regarding creative rights, are undeniably important, our concerns must extend far beyond these tip-of-the-iceberg issues. As it pertains to synthetic media such as deepfakes, voice replication, and the like, the heart of the issue goes beyond digital citizenship. It's about *citizenship*, period. It's about personal rights and freedoms being challenged as reality is distorted to fit a narrative that blackmails *Black males*. Moreover, there is a risk that synthetic media could perpetuate our reliance on exploitative practices within the prison industrial complex. In light of the existing school-to-prison pipeline, AI has the potential to accelerate the US's position as a global leader in incarcerating its own citizens.

KS:

One of the many areas I tend to focus on in my talks is the importance of representation. We often shape our views of ourselves and the possibilities we hold by how we see ourselves represented. It goes far beyond just representation and connects to things such as self-esteem, dismantling stereotypes, affirmations, and validations. With the continued growth and growing availability of artificial intelligence platforms, the need for teaching, learning, and expanding our work around media literacy becomes even more essential. I really like how the National Association for Media Literacy Education essentially defines media literacy within their mission statement, "the ability to access, analyze, evaluate, create, and act using all forms of communication."[49] Many of us remember the early days of Google search. You would enter a query and within seconds you would get a page of links to then click on. What wasn't happening enough was developing a process for vetting that information for its reliability, credibility, and usability. For those of us that have been around for a while, we used to cite a few websites that contained fake information solely for the purpose of demonstrating you can put anything on the internet. In fact, a certain demographic of the educator population may remember the Pacific Northwest tree octopus.[50] If you are not familiar with this reference it was a very popular website that was an internet hoax. It was created for the purpose of demonstrating you can create and publish anything on the internet.

Thus, the reason our need for media literacy is rapidly becoming essential is due to the growth of platforms that can create synthetic media. The better it gets, the harder it will be to discern real from fake, fact from fiction, or even worse, truth from lies. This is becoming enough of a concern that in the state of California two recent Senate bills have been ratified explicitly identifying the need to incorporate media literacy across grade levels and content areas.[51] How do we effectively discern the differences between **misinformation, disinformation,** *and* **malinformation***? Two very close friends of mine, Jennifer LaGarde and Darren Hudgins, published the book,* Developing Digital Detectives.[52] *In it they talk about the different lenses in which we view, consume, and interact with media. They are our trigger lens, access lens, forensic lens, and motive lens. As different artificial intelligence platforms grow and get better our need for media literacy increases and our processes for vetting media will need to iterate as well.*

Understanding the motivations behind deepfake creation is crucial. Take, for instance, the hypothetical scenario of generating dialogue for existing video footage. While this could be used for positive purposes, such as restoring historical recordings or creating accessible educational materials, it could also be exploited for malicious ends, such as fabricating political speeches or spreading misinformation.

Therefore, it is essential we consider both sides of the coin. What are the potential benefits of AI-generated content? Could it be used to bridge communication gaps, enhance artistic expression, or preserve cultural heritage? Alternatively, what are the potential harms? Could deepfakes be weaponized to damage reputations, sow discord, or manipulate public opinion?

We need robust frameworks to identify and flag potentially harmful content, holding creators and distributors accountable for their work's downstream effects. Transparency and user education are crucial. Equipping individuals with the ability to critically analyze information empowers them to recognize the deceptive nature of deepfakes. The road ahead presents significant challenges, but the potential consequences of inaction are severe. It is imperative that we navigate this new frontier with a balance of optimism and caution, harnessing the power of AI while acknowledging and mitigating its inherent risks. Only through this approach can we ensure that this technology serves humanity, rather than becoming a tool for manipulation.

Protecting Students: Dangers of Deepfakes in Education

The implications of unchecked synthetic media are particularly perilous for marginalized student groups. Students of color already face systemic biases and barriers to opportunity. The emergence of deepfakes raises alarming risks of further perpetuating harmful stereotypes, silencing minority voices, and sowing seeds of distrust through manipulated media. We have a profound responsibility as educators to safeguard our students against such misuse of technology. This imperative demands a proactive, multifaceted approach. First and foremost, we need to prioritize media literacy, equipping students with the skills to identify manipulated content and approach online information with discernment.

Equally crucial is cultivating a climate of open dialogue where creativity and self-expression flourish without fear of suspicion. Students should feel empowered to harness technology ethically, rather than feel ostracized by its potential pitfalls. Far too often there are educators who spurn a student's use of available resources due to a number of factors, including some that are self-imposed. One being a lack of interest or intent to learn due to prioritizing comfort over growth. It's like Linus, from Peanuts, refusing to allow himself to ever be separated from his blanket. The comfort of predictability and control is more important than the possibility and the liberation. Fostering critical perspectives and mutual understanding through classroom discourse is key. Furthermore, transparency and strong accountability mechanisms must be embedded into the development pipeline of synthetic media technologies. Community-centered design thinking can help mitigate harmful biases. Ongoing audits and impact assessments can flag potential misuses.

Protecting vulnerable student groups from misinformation and manipulation will require sustained collective action. But guided by moral conviction and vigilance, we can turn the tide, ensuring synthetic media serves as a force for democratizing creativity, not for injustice. A glaring vulnerability lies in the unchecked spread of manipulated media targeting marginalized student groups. Deepfakes depicting minority students or public figures with manufactured content could rapidly proliferate online, sowing misinformation and discord before interventions occur.

Speed is of the essence in detecting and halting such malicious disinformation. Educators, school administrators and tech platforms must establish rapid response protocols. Proactive media literacy campaigns can immunize audiences preemptively against manipulated content. Lawmakers must update policies to hold distributors accountable. Equally vital is dismantling the underlying biases that fuel abuse of synthetic media. Positive representations in curriculums, constructive discourse around diversity, and teaching the multifaceted heritage of marginalized groups helps counter one-dimensional stereotypes. Deepfakes thrive on exploiting ignorance; knowledge is their kryptonite.

Safeguarding students demands sustained collective action, not piecemeal interventions. Through comprehensive education, strong governance, research-driven technology development, and upholding ethical principles, we can mitigate risks and foster responsible innovation. Our students deserve nothing less. A significant vulnerability lies in the absence of transparency and oversight in synthetic media development. Most deepfake algorithms are **black boxes**, trained on opaque datasets by anonymous creators. This shadowy landscape enables unethical use like political sabotage or slander.

Rigorous audits, impact assessments, and accountability structures must be mandated before deploying synthetic media tools, especially in public education. Their inner workings and capabilities should be transparent, not obscured. Schools and educators partnering with tech firms must demand full evaluative access and ethical development practices. Furthermore, the law must evolve to catch up with technological change. Outdated policies leave manipulative deepfakes in a nebulous gray area. Lawmakers must future-proof regulations to prohibit malicious uses while allowing creative innovation under a framework of informed consent. Supporting research around detection can also help curb harms.

Protecting vulnerable students demands sustained vigilance through education, compassionate culture-building, corporate responsibility, dynamic policies and a commitment to justice. With comprehensive action, we can promote ethical synthetic media, turning possibility into progress. A significant aspect of protection is psychological and emotional support. Seeing manipulated images of oneself or one's community can inflict deep trauma, especially for students of color facing systemic biases. Counselors and educators need trauma-informed training to help students process and contextualize deepfakes.

Building student resilience is also crucial. Classroom exercises teaching self-affirmation, overcoming self-doubt, and fostering peer support systems can inoculate against gaslighting, which is the act of psychological manipulation often for insidious reasons leading one to question their reality and increased periods of self-doubt. Activities exploring one's identity, values, and strengths ground students in their self-worth. Vulnerability around sharing common struggles can unite diverse peer groups. Equally vital is cultivating student agency. Synthetic media can make one feel powerless, but activities that allow students to create positive content as a collective voice restore agency. Student-led campaigns against misinformation using counter-messaging also help combat false narratives. Their active participation turns vulnerability into empowerment. A holistic approach addressing both preventative education and trauma response is needed. From emotional support to resilience building and elevating authentic student voices, schools can help turn pain into purpose, fears into action, and threats into opportunities for growth.

Teaching Awareness: Identifying and Mitigating Fake Media

As schools integrate synthetic media tools, a top priority must be collaboration with students. This collaboration should focus on developing media literacy skills to identify manipulated content and analyze sources critically. Together, schools and students should co-design ethical guidelines for synthetic media use, balancing creative freedom with the prevention of harassment and misrepresentation. Empowering students to co-design policies and lead presentations on creating a safe learning environment will build a culture of responsibility. Learning about the potential and misuse of synthetic media should not be solely a top-down directive. By actively participating, students gain a deeper understanding of the technology and its implications, enabling responsible use.

In order to pull this off, curriculums need to blend technical skills with critical thinking. Students need to understand how AI generates synthetic media in order to identify artifacts, such as areas of an image that is AI generated and has abnormalities like extra fingers, arms that do not line up, too many teeth, or areas in which the color and lighting are clearly not in sync. But open-ended discussions exploring synthetic media's societal impact are equally important for developing citizenship. A balanced, holistic approach ensures students use the tools of tomorrow wisely. As schools navigate this complex landscape, wisdom must guide their steps. With student wellbeing, equity, and ethics at the helm, synthetic media can become a springboard for digital literacy, media discernment, and responsible innovation. But without awareness at its core, this promising frontier risks becoming a vector for misinformation and manipulation.

Developing source evaluation skills is essential. Students must learn to question where information originates, who authored it, and what their intentions are. Scrutinizing metadata—timestamps, geotags, and digital watermarks— offers clues about a source's legitimacy. Students should trace claims to primary sources instead of accepting chains of reposts, cultivating healthy skepticism in the process. Hands-on projects raise the stakes and tap into student interests. Let's say a hot-button topic emerges, like Drake using AI-generated voices of Tupac and Snoop Dogg in a diss track aimed at Kendrick Lamar. This becomes the launchpad for a critical dialogue. Students can choose a side and debate the ethics of using AI to resurrect voices for artistic expression. But before they can argue their case, they need the tools to discern truth from fiction.

Now, the real learning kicks in. Students delve into techniques used to manipulate audio. They analyze spectrograms, which visually represent sound waves, to identify inconsistencies. They learn about deepfake detection algorithms and their limitations. Peer review of student-created synthetic media outputs provides practical experience in spotting inconsistencies. The Drake diss track example becomes a springboard for broader discussions. Analyzing real-world examples like political deepfakes ignites discussions about manipulated media's impact on elections and social movements. Nurturing an ethical mindset is equally important. Present scenarios with ethical gray areas, such as using AI to recreate a deceased actor's voice for a biopic. This sharpens critical thinking skills. Guiding questions force students to explore creative dilemmas from multiple perspectives with empathy. Class contracts on ethical technology use build a sense of collective responsibility. By weaving relevant pop culture references and student interests into the curriculum, you create a dynamic learning environment where critical thinking thrives.

We envision a holistic approach where every rightsholder plays a vital role in preparing students to be savvy media consumers and collaborators in AI policy development. This means reimagining passive classrooms and empowering student voices. Students take the lead, conducting peer workshops to teach authentication skills, and spreading awareness through viral anti-deepfake campaigns. Educators evolve into facilitators, receiving training to navigate complex discussions around the ethical and societal impact of synthetic media. Counselors gain specialized protocols to offer trauma-informed support for those targeted by harmful manipulated media. Administrators champion school-wide media literacy campaigns, actively revising policies with student feedback while forging partnerships with tech firms to fund educational initiatives and shape ethical design. Outreach to families reinforces media literacy concepts and empowers them to join this societal movement. Ongoing evaluation and improvement create a constantly evolving media literacy environment, with student feedback driving curriculum changes and surveys quantifying the impact of these efforts.

As AI tools continuously evolve, we are required to sharpen our skills in identifying inaccuracies and inauthenticities. We acknowledge that synthetic media literacy isn't a destination, but an ongoing journey. Navigating this ever-shifting landscape requires agility, collaboration, and a commitment to lifelong learning for all rightsholders. Only then can we uphold our shared responsibility to foster generations equipped to navigate the digital world responsibly and empowered with their own authentic voices.

The rise of AI-generated synthetic media in education creates a double-edged sword. As these tools become ubiquitous, schools have a critical role to play in equipping students with the knowledge to navigate them effectively and ethically. However, education alone isn't enough. Protecting vulnerable student groups demands a holistic societal approach. This means holding tech companies accountable for ethical synthetic media development by implementing safeguards that prevent the creation of harmful deepfakes. We need dynamic policies from governments focused on transparency, user control, and bias mitigation in AI algorithms. These measures work together to safeguard human dignity while fostering creative innovation.

The road ahead is undeniably complex, riddled with challenges that lack easy answers. Yet, with wisdom, empathy, and an unwavering commitment to justice as our guiding lights, we can make a transformative difference. Through collective action and unwavering diligence, we can empower generations to harness the potential of synthetic media, expanding the horizons of human creativity and understanding for all. This is especially critical for Black and

Brown students, who make up a significant portion of the student population in urban schools.[53] These students are uniquely vulnerable to the perils of synthetic media. Deepfakes and manipulated content can be used to spread misinformation that reinforces negative stereotypes, further marginalizing these groups.

Media literacy is not just about protection, it's about empowerment. By ensuring all students, especially those from marginalized backgrounds, have the tools to navigate this digital landscape, we can break down systemic barriers and open doors to new opportunities. Our students deserve nothing less than the chance to be active participants in shaping the future of synthetic media, not simply passive consumers or disempowered victims.

CHAPTER 6

Student Data, AI Power

Collecting and Controlling: Student Data to Train AI Systems

KS:

One of the most common questions I used to pose when it came to speaking with educators about different platforms and applications was, "Did you read the Terms of Service (TOS) or the End User Licensing Agreement (EULA)?" I did this because there were so many platforms that had terms forbidding the sharing of information such as your username and password. Yet, educators would still share these, including with students, for a variety of reasons including ensuring access for their students since the platform was either restricted, financially inaccessible to their school or district, inaccessible outside of school, or flat out blocked without any rational justification.

Over the years that set of questions has evolved to things like, "Who owns your data?" "What are they doing with your information/data?" "If you upload a photo, who owns your image and your likeness?" "How long do they own it?" The reasons I bring this up now are twofold. The TOS and EULA are lengthy—very lengthy—and filled with legalese an educator would need to add a law degree to their schooling in order to fully comprehend. Reading through either would be like sitting through the end credits of a movie. Unless you are a hardcore Marvel Cinematic Universe fan—if you know you know—there is little chance you will remain seated all the way through the scrolling of the end credits.

So rather than carefully navigating a sea of legal jargon, attempting to make sense of that which is designed to obfuscate, I have a simple tactic. I would go to the relevant TOS/EULA page and keystroke "command or control F," which means find on page. The terms I would always use in my "find on page" search are image, likeness, term, and ownership. This would filter through the content and take me to all instances where these words appear in the TOS or EULA. That way I could more easily determine if the use of that application or platform may or may not compromise something I didn't want it to. This is one of several strategies I deem necessary in order to take an information literacy approach to using a platform/application. Now with the advent of generative artificial intelligence, there is a more streamlined approach. More on that to come.

Before delving into the specifics of this chapter, it's important to establish a shared understanding of data regulation, policy, and the laws protecting student information. Key regulations include the **Children's Online Privacy Protection Act (COPPA)**, the **Family Educational Rights and Privacy Act (FERPA)**, and the **European Union's General Data Protection Regulation (GDPR)**. These frameworks are essential for navigating the use of AI in education.

A common misconception is that AI automatically violates data protection regulations like FERPA. This is not the case. FERPA primarily focuses on protecting **personally identifiable information** (**PII**) like report cards and attendance records—it doesn't directly prohibit the use of AI. When using AI in education, it's vital to ask: What specific AI technology am I using, and how does it process student data? Why am I using this tool, and does the purpose justify the use of potentially sensitive student information? Rashly blocking AI due to potential privacy concerns undermines a crucial facet of digital citizenship—responsible technology usage. This requires robust policies, practical support, and a clear understanding of data practices beyond regulations like COPPA. For instance, opting for a regular Gmail account exposes data that a Google Workspace for Education domain securely protects.

When considering AI platforms, especially popular LLMs, resist the urge to either demonize them or assume digital natives instinctively know their safe use. Instead, implement structured guidance. Equip students with the knowledge to avoid divulging PII while interacting with LLMs. This emphasizes the need for an ethics framework within education. Students must develop the ability to discern ethical actions, while educators and administrators require support to navigate potential pitfalls. Uploading a student roster to an AI tool for tasks based on demographics, for example, demands careful consideration and ethical principles. Ultimately, our goal extends beyond mere algorithms and data points. We strive to harness the power of AI while upholding ethical principles and safeguarding student privacy. This translates to not just diversifying learning groups or randomizing teams, but also ensuring that AI-powered tools enhance education equitably and responsibly.

Privacy in the face of powerful algorithms requires equally clear-eyed scrutiny. Are we sacrificing long-term privacy benefits for short-term convenience or novelty? Consider the allure of AI apps, for example, that morph photos or predict appearances. While seemingly harmless, their hidden costs might be alarming. By uploading seemingly innocent images, users often unknowingly surrender perpetual rights to their likeness. Is it fair or realistic to expect students and educators to dissect lengthy legalese? Shouldn't platforms be upfront about what they require, highlighting key points in layman's terms?

While AI offers enticing opportunities to streamline tasks, it is an absolute necessity that we pause and consider the potential surrender of personal information. In the rush for convenience, we might inadvertently relinquish critical data to third-party AI tools, leaving its fate and usage shrouded in uncertainty. Here's an engaging exercise that empowers both educators and students to become more responsible AI users. Start by copying and pasting the Privacy Policy and Terms and Conditions for any AI application you use, whether it's for educational purposes or otherwise. As previously stated, use an LLM of your choice and insert this prompt: "Act as an intellectual property lawyer and add, 'with special interests in AI ethics.' Review these terms and conditions and share your concerns. Explain it on a fifth-grade/year five level."

Imagine having a lawyer who specializes in AI ethics readily available to answer your questions! While AI isn't perfect, and there's always a risk of encountering false information in the form of hallucinations, this exercise can be a valuable first step. To enhance the accuracy of your "AI lawyer's" analysis, consider running the same query through multiple LLMs. Additionally, traditional fact-checking methods remain crucial. Use the "find" function (Ctrl or Cmd + F) to search for key terms within the privacy policy. This initial "AI lawyer" analysis will equip you to identify potential areas of concern within the privacy policy. Armed with these questions, you can then reach out to the AI application's developers via email or social media for further clarification. By taking these steps, you become a more empowered user of AI technology. You'll be better equipped to make informed decisions about the AI tools you use and the data you share.

This notion of "AI auditing AI" extends beyond individual users. Imagine a central repository, accessible to educators and parents, where different AI platforms can be analyzed and compared based on their **data provenance**, **algorithmic biases**, and privacy implications. Such a resource would shine a light on the inner workings of these tools, enabling educators to make informed choices about their integration within educational settings. Cultivating a culture of critical inquiry, promoting informed user engagement, and harnessing the power of AI to deconstruct its own complexities, we can navigate the AI labyrinth with confidence. This journey towards responsible technology integration requires acknowledging potential pitfalls, equipping ourselves with the tools to understand them, and ultimately, turning the tables on AI, using it to empower rather than exploit.

Remember, your computer acts as a bridge to the digital world. Our point isn't to advocate for digital abstinence; children already leave digital traces through their online activities. The true challenge lies in empowering them to recognize the implications of these actions. For instance, uploading a TikTok video or a picture with friends might not seem like a conscious data exchange, yet these seemingly insignificant acts can contribute to the vast datasets fueling AI platforms, large language models, and image generators. That picture? It's highly likely to become part of the training data for these innovative tools.

Within the educational realm, we can guide students by emphasizing media literacy principles. We can say, "Here's what you need to know about the potential consequences of your online actions, and here's what might be hidden within this specific tool." This awareness serves as a catalyst for critical thinking. A teacher's advice against sharing personal information in a large language model, due to potential dataset integration, prompts the question: What other information have we unknowingly surrendered to the digital landscape? This focus on media literacy is crucial as AI continues to permeate our world in often surprising ways. As we often emphasize in our workshops, even the familiar spell-checker in Microsoft Word (remember Clippy?) is a form of AI. Our tools today are similar to those of yesterday, only smarter.

Autocorrect tools relied on limited **datasets** to catch basic errors. With the rise of the internet, a vast amount of data became available, allowing autocorrect to learn from common phrases and patterns found online. This, combined with the development of AI, enabled it to analyze user behavior to some extent. While some features might personalize suggestions based on frequently used words, recognizing the nuances of writing style is less common. Now, with the advent of generative AI, entire sentences can be formulated based on the previous sentence written. In addition, AI is now able to show suggestions on how to reword your sentences and give explanations for the changes, acting as a low-key personalized writing tutor as you write. As this technology advances and specialized tools for education mature, AI will play an increasingly important role in shaping educational experiences.

As AI strides confidently into the realm of education-specific platforms, school systems and districts must stand as vigilant guardians of student data. Armed with robust digital usage policies and a keen understanding of regulations like COPPA, educators and administrators have a duty to demand accountability from the technology they choose. Before signing on the dotted line for any AI-powered platform, schools and school systems must ask crucial questions: What data sets does it use (source data)? What data does it collect? How does it use that data? Is any data collected to train the model? Who owns the data? Are data cleansing measures in place? And what happens to the student information it inevitably gathers from classrooms and across the district?

Silence or evasiveness in response to questions about data collection should be a red flag. In this realm, transparency is paramount. Students, teachers, parents, and the entire school community deserve to know exactly what data is being collected, who controls it (the school district, the AI vendor, or a third party), who has access (teachers, administrators, or external entities), and its ultimate fate (used for internal purposes, anonymized and sold, or something else entirely). Understanding data retention policies is also crucial. Will the data be stored indefinitely, or are there procedures in place for secure deletion after a set period?

Only with this comprehensive knowledge can informed decisions be made about the AI tools that shape our educational landscape. This is why it is vital that we weigh the potential benefits of AI against the risks associated with data collection and use. Consider a seemingly helpful education app designed to assist teachers with lesson planning. This app may allow other companies to track user behavior, including "third parties that deliver content or offers" (i.e., marketing). Worse yet, the app's privacy policy might state that its provisions can change "at any time for any reason," without directly notifying users. This lack of transparency and control significantly risks violating regulations such as FERPA, where schools and districts must maintain authority along with ensure protections over how student data is used and disclosed.

However, the discussion of data privacy goes beyond regulations like COPPA and FERPA. **The Protection of Pupil Rights Amendment (PPRA)** also plays vital roles in safeguarding student information. If you've never heard of PPRA, you're welcome! In particular, PPRA ensures transparency when institutions request student data for federally funded surveys or evaluations.[54] This is especially crucial when considering the questionable efficacy of many high-stakes tests that fail to predict future student success. The question then arises: Why prioritize assessments that generate financial gain for corporations while offering little value to students and institutions?

The answer, unfortunately, often lies in a tangled web of financial interests and power dynamics. Major US corporations like McGraw-Hill, Houghton Mifflin Harcourt, and Pearson dominate the lucrative standardized testing market, fueled by hundreds of millions in federal funding to develop assessments mandated by legislation like No Child Left Behind.[55] This lack of transparency is unacceptable. Parents, educators, and institutions deserve to know the truth about the data collected, its destinations, and its uses. For example, what data is used to determine the types of questions used in a standardized assessment? From whose perspective and based on what experience? What is the purpose behind having sections of a standardized assessment with 60 questions but only 50 are actually scored? What data is being tabulated on the exams, and used for future exams, that often leads to the predictability of scoring largely based on the zip code of the school? Teachers are usually required to sign an affidavit acknowledging the duty, when administering exams, to maintain the exams integrity. Yet this very same approach remains shrouded in secrecy when it comes to answering the previously posed questions.

Yet, transparency alone is not enough. When schools present parents and guardians with documents or emails brimming with technical jargon, confusion and passivity often prevail. The fear of the unknown can easily silence objections to potential data misuse. Therefore, schools have a higher responsibility to translate complex information into clear, accessible language. Warnings and precautions should be presented upfront, not hidden in dense legalese. Hiding behind murky terminology is a tactic often employed by those with vested interests in circumventing scrutiny. Again, this is where the previously suggested prompt becomes helpful: … explain on a fifth grade reading level. Where technical terms create confusion, AI can bring clarity.

The demand for accountability extends beyond the classroom walls and into the digital tools we choose for education. We can recall the initial resistance to Google Apps, particularly Google Docs, fueled by concerns about data security. However, much of this resistance stemmed from a lack of concrete information and an atmosphere of fear mongering.

Take, for instance, the concerns surrounding uploading Individualized Education Programs (IEPs) and 504 plans to Google Docs. For any of our non-US educators reading this book, IEPs are legal documents outlining the specific needs and accommodations required for students with disabilities to succeed in school.[56] While printed IEPs left on teachers' desks pose a significant security risk, a secure, cloud-based solution, coupled with robust data protection measures, could offer greater accessibility and protection for these crucial documents. The key lies in shifting the focus from fear to informed decisions. Instead of simply fearing the unknown, we simply need to ask the right questions. This applies not only to cloud-based storage but also to the emerging use of AI in education.

One pressing question is: Is it ethical to use AI to assist with IEP generation? If so, what information should be anonymized or excluded to ensure ethical use? Furthermore, how can we mitigate potential biases within the data used by AI to ensure equity in the generated IEPs? By asking these critical questions and demanding clear answers from AI developers, we can navigate the ethical use of AI in education. The integration of AI into education is inevitable, but it should not come at the cost of student privacy or ethical transparency. By demanding accountability, asking the right questions, and fostering open communication, we can ensure that technology empowers learning and strengthens our communities, not exploits them. The future of education depends on it.

Transparency and clear communication should be the bedrock of data handling practices. This extends beyond occasional discussions during conferences or group meetings. Regularly reviewing and clarifying information ensures continuous understanding of the contractual agreements associated with online platforms. Parents deserve clear, easily accessible information about how their children's data is managed, and it should be readily available for ongoing comprehension.

Privacy Concerns: Risks and Harms From using Student Data

Back in the day, clicking "allow" felt harmless—our limited imagination and the technology of the time couldn't grasp the full scope of data usage. In fact, a few things to ponder, are you aware of how browser cookies work? When the permissions for enabling cookies pops up, do you just click "accept all" or do you go into the selection menu and ensure only "performance and functionality" are selected? Ever wonder what happens and what the potential effects are of clicking "accept all?"

Let's start with building an understanding of what cookies are—of course a famous blue character wouldn't be so eager as to want these types of cookies. Cookies are like little notes or tags that a website puts on your computer. The purpose is for a website to essentially remember who you are. Ever go to a shopping website, put a few things in your cart, leave the website, and then return remembering you forgot to complete the transaction? But miraculously the items are still in the cart—that happened because of browser cookies. In most cases, these cookies are stored in your browser and remain there unless you either manually clear them out or enable a browser setting to clear them out at a specific time interval.

Cookies generally have three main goals: remembering who you are for login purposes, personalizing your experience, and tracking what you do to provide targeted ads. When you click "accept all" the potential consequences are a loss of privacy, more ads that are further personalized, and potential collection of your data. Now, with AI advancements surging, the potential for our information to be not just used, but weaponized, is staggering. AI tools promise powerful assistants, but at a cost: they predict your words and serve ads based on years of your online trail— clicks, purchases, calendars, emails, even subject lines. All this personal data, sacrificed on the altar of targeted advertising, serves as a stark reminder. Technology can leverage our past data for good or for bad. Therefore, it is crucial we empower individuals—not just with awareness, but with the ability to understand the significance of their data and retain control over it, both now and in the future.

Fostering an ongoing dialogue about personal data, consent, and rights is an essential step in building trust in the digital age. Education and awareness empower individuals to make informed choices about their data, safeguarding their privacy and promoting responsible data use within our educational institutions. Only through transparency, accountability, and informed consent can we navigate the challenges and opportunities presented by student data in the digital age. Understanding the intricacies of any technology is key to responsible use, and AI is no exception. In this realm, three critical areas demand our attention:

1. Demystifying the Design: The first step towards informed engagement is understanding the origins and functions of the AI platform. Who built it? What are its intended purposes? What user data does it require to operate? Transparency from providers is paramount. If they cannot or will not answer these fundamental questions, doubts about the platform's suitability for educational contexts are justified and warranted.

2. Public Trust and Public Funds: When public tax dollars are used to fund an AI platform shrouded in secrecy, concerns about accountability naturally arise. Resources entrusted to educators and institutions for the public good deserve responsible management and open communication. Failure to demonstrate transparency in data use and platform operation raises serious questions about the ethical and financial implications of such investments.

3. Embracing Transparency as an Ethical Imperative: Ultimately, the issue of transparency transcends

125

technical concerns and lands firmly within the realm of ethics. Students, parents, educators, and the broader community deserve to understand how their data is being collected, utilized, and protected within the AI ecosystem. Clear communication regarding data practices is not just a technical necessity; it is a fundamental ethical obligation, ensuring that the integration of AI in education serves the learning needs of all rightsholders without compromising their rights and privacy. Neither is transparency solely an individual responsibility. As Dr. Timnit Gebru states, "What I've realized is that we can talk about the ethics and fairness of AI all we want, but if our institutions don't allow for this kind of work to take place, then it won't. At the end of the day, this needs to be about institutional and structural change."[57]

The rise of AI demands a proactive approach to technology use in schools. This requires a united effort from educators, administrators, and the entire school community, especially parents and caregivers. In education, we often focus on "essential questions." As instructional coaches and administrator advisors, we challenge ourselves by asking, "Who does this benefit, and what purpose does it serve?" Applying this critical thinking to AI privacy is crucial. By empowering students and teachers to ask key questions like "What data is collected? How is it used? Who has access?" and "Who owns the data?" we can spark a vital dialogue. This approach can push back against companies prioritizing profit over user protection, expediency over efficacy. Furthermore, education technology developers may be compelled to prioritize ethical practices in their documentation, moving them from the fine print to the forefront. When the entire education community unifies to raise privacy concerns, businesses are pressured towards greater transparency and potentially even changing their practices. This is part of a multi-tiered ethical approach we are compelled by circumstance to insist upon.

School and district leaders have a dual responsibility here. They must actively seek answers to these critical questions, but also proactively provide transparent information before concerns even arise. This proactive approach demonstrates a commitment to responsible AI implementation, reassuring rightsholders (students, parents, educators) that the potential benefits outweigh any potential risks. Treading carefully is key as we venture into the AI frontier of education. Prioritizing transparency, demanding accountability, and fostering informed engagement are crucial to ensure this powerful technology empowers positive change and equitable learning, not jeopardizes student privacy or ethical principles. Equipping users— students in this case—to understand and leverage these tools while safeguarding their digital well-being is paramount. Organizations like the Technical University of Munich are pioneering the way with scenario-based instruction that sparks discussions on AI ethics in education.[58] While concrete examples of AI ethics literacy programs may be scarce due to the rapid rise of AI, we are called upon to rise to the challenge. Responsible and thoughtful navigation of the AI landscape is essential for the future of education.

In the education realm, integrating powerful AI tools necessitates a nuanced approach. While its potential to personalize learning and unlock new possibilities is undeniable, navigating ethical challenges and safeguarding user rights are paramount. Achieving this requires a paradigm shift, moving beyond static concepts like "good digital citizens," far too often applied in a power dynamic context, questioning who determines what this "citizenship" entails and from what perspective. Therefore, we have a duty to embrace a more dynamic framework empowering individuals as active participants in shaping the rules governing our digital lives. The so-called citizens, the students themselves, must be involved in creating this new digital democracy.

Transparency from the companies that make the tools and deep understanding and consent from caregivers lies at the heart of this new vision. We can and must prioritize clarity and accountability. The emphasis should shift from ambiguous, subjective frameworks to explicit rules governing AI use within school districts, assessing whether policies align with existing laws and whether terms of service clearly outline data collection and usage practices. These critical questions demand clear, unambiguous answers.

Open dialogue and diverse perspectives are vital in navigating this ever-evolving landscape. By prioritizing transparency, accountability, and informed consent, we can ensure that AI serves as a force for good in education, empowering learning without compromising ethical principles or individual rights. Let us collaborate to navigate a transparent and ethical path through the digital landscape, guaranteeing that all rights holders thrive in this new age of technological innovations. This democratic approach extends beyond mere information consumption. Students, parents, and educators must be active rightsholders in decision-making processes, not just passive recipients of policies. While town halls can be valuable for gathering opinions, they often fail to provide the necessary platform for meaningful participation. Instead, imagine committees composed of students, caregivers, and educators working collaboratively. Design-thinking activities involving representation from all rightsholders that result in collaborative goal setting are what we're after. If a recommended protocol for design thinking through real-world problems is needed, *Solve in Time!* (developed by Lanier in 2022) is recommended.[59] However, the process for isolating these real and relevant processes comes second to ensuring the right people are at the table. These diverse voices, united in a shared goal, can lead to better understanding, consensus, and ultimately, more effective policies governing technology use in schools.

Preparing students for active citizenship in the digital world involves equipping them with the knowledge and skills they need to navigate its complexities. This includes understanding the legal landscape, their rights and responsibilities, and the delicate dance of data exchange inherent in using digital tools. By empowering students with this knowledge, we can foster accountability from the very companies that create these tools. However, this journey requires recognizing the irreversible nature of technological harm. Once a data breach occurs, the genie cannot be put back in the bottle. Stolen information, once unleashed, cannot be truly retrieved. This underscores the critical urgency for proactive measures. Our emphasis should be on prevention, not mitigation. It is of essential significance that we prioritize robust data protection systems and empower users to understand and safeguard their digital rights and information. This proactive approach forms the cornerstone of responsible technology integration in education. Promoting active participation in policymaking, equipping individuals with media literacy skills, and prioritizing data security, we can navigate the digital landscape with confidence, ensuring that technology empowers learning without compromising ethical principles or user rights.

Taking Charge: Student Data Rights and Responsibilities

One key line of inquiry focuses on the platform's creators. Who crafted this technology? Beyond the names and titles, understanding the diversity of the development team—in terms of race, socio-economic background, education, gender identity, and even geographical location—sheds light on the perspectives that shaped the platform. A homogenous team might overlook nuances and biases invisible to their shared experience. Next, we have to scrutinize the data that fuels the AI engine. Where does it originate? What narratives does it encode? As Dr. Joy Buolamwini explains in her book, *Unmasking AI*, she emphasizes the concept of "the coded gaze," which refers to the biases and discrimination that can be embedded in technology products. AI development often resembles crafting a new book from borrowed library volumes, most notably, existing datasets and models, which can be sourced from various places including open-source repositories like GitHub.[60]

To provide further analysis on this point, visualize yourself walking into a library. You cast your gaze on all the stacks of books. All the different representations of story, experience, and ideas. It is vast and at times overwhelming. You then go to the library desk where our information hero, your friendly neighborhood librarian, guides you to an area in the library based upon your need and/or interest. The need you have is to get started writing fictional narratives. Your goal is to build a collection of your own fictional narratives for later publication. You "source" your ideas and even overall story collection structure based on the books you review in the library. The library is your go to place to source, curate, learn, and in some cases share your stories and ideas. This is what GitHub essentially is for developers. Now imagine being able to do this as one of your primary sources for building an AI platform. Additional sourced data will likely come from the API (**Application Programming Interface**) of an existing large language model. The information gleaned from existing datasets forms the foundation upon which new systems are built.

At the heart of every AI platform lies a hidden story: the data and code that serve as its building blocks. Understanding the origin of these ingredients—the datasets and code used for training—is akin to unearthing the provenance of food on our plates. Just as locally sourced vegetables and organically raised meats tell a tale of sustainable practices, the source of an AI's data reveals its potential biases and harmful effects that often go unchecked or unnoticed. Asking critical questions about these aspects—their origin, current usage, and future acquisition plans—empowers us to anticipate potential issues and proactively develop strategies for mitigation.

Herein lies the potential for perpetuating biases. Just as a flawed recipe will yield an unsatisfactory dish, data tainted by prejudice will yield AI that reflects and amplifies those biases. Understanding the source and nature of the datasets employed is therefore crucial for holding AI platforms accountable and ensuring they operate with fairness and equity. Imagine the development process akin to preparing a traditional Italian meal. No chef cultivates every ingredient from scratch; instead, they rely on the quality and diversity of what's available. Tomatoes, garlic, basil, onions—each contribute its unique essence to the final dish. Similarly, programmers utilize existing datasets as the raw materials for their AI creations. By examining the "grocery list" of data sources, we can identify potential contaminants and ensure the dish that emerges is one of inclusivity and ethical responsibility.

Through persistent inquiry and a critical eye, we can peel back the layers of opaqueness surrounding AI development. By scrutinizing the creators, the data, and the underlying processes, we empower ourselves to navigate the digital landscape with informed vigilance, ensuring that AI serves as a tool for progress, not a reflection of our biases.

The naivety surrounding free platforms, with their alluring bells and whistles, deserves a reality check. The adage, "if it's free, you are the product," rings true, especially when it comes to AI tools. To gain a clearer picture of the privacy implications associated with these seemingly costless offerings, delving into the often-opaque terms of service is crucial. Scrutinizing key terms like "image," "likeness," "ownership," and "duration" or "term" can reveal the hidden costs of our digital engagement, shedding light on the rights we surrender with each click and swipe. For example, if you upload your own image, voice, or writing, who owns the output, you or the service? Further, have you just granted the right to use your likeness for an indefinite period, potentially in perpetuity?

However, our aim is not to demonize AI or discourage its use altogether. As a matter of fact, we utilize and are big proponents of the free AI offerings of Google, Microsoft, Anthropic, and others. We utilize them and encourage schools to consider them and a diversity of other tools to gain a better understanding of how these different tools work and to utilize them more effectively. We recognize the advantages of using free tools to encourage equity by ensuring everyone has access to robust features, regardless of their ability to pay for premium subscriptions typically priced at $20 or more per month. Nonetheless, we also recognize the need to always critique the terms and conditions and consider the ethical implications of using platforms that make their features prominent but intentionally hide how they may own and use your data in the long term. We acknowledge its immense potential to revolutionize education, but without proper understanding and responsible deployment, these benefits can be overshadowed by ethical concerns. Our objective is to empower users to harness the power of AI thoughtfully, navigating its complexities with informed awareness.

Therefore, our message in the final chapter of this book advocates for a balanced approach. While acknowledging the risks inherent in AI, we highlight the empowering tools at our disposal, such as AI-powered terms of service analysis. By equipping users with these tools and fostering a culture of critical inquiry, we can unlock the true potential of AI, shaping a future where technology empowers rather than exploits. In the intricate realm of education, the integration of powerful tools like AI demands a nuanced approach. While its potential to personalize learning and unlock new possibilities is undeniable, navigating the ethical challenges and safeguarding user rights are paramount.

By fostering informed engagement and open communication among all rightsholders, we can ensure the responsible and equitable use of AI in education. Students, parents, educators, administrators, and technology providers each play a crucial role. Collectively examining the origins, objectives, and data practices behind AI tools enables us to make wise choices, upholding both innovation and ethical principles. Empowering users with knowledge is key, from understanding privacy regulations to leveraging AI itself to demystify opaque terms of service. Moving beyond fear, we have the ability to equip individuals with the necessary skills to protect their rights and make conscious decisions about their data. This ability to exercise agency amidst powerful technologies is itself a hallmark of digital citizenship. As AI's presence grows, its unfolding narrative will be authored collectively through our choices and actions. Our shared destiny depends on writing this story well.

CHAPTER 7

Toward More Equitable Classroom AI

KS:

"There is a lot we can learn about social media's unregulated evolution over the past decade that directly applies to AI companies and technologies. These lessons can help us avoid making the same mistakes with AI that we did with social media," data scientist Nathan Sanders and security technologist Bruce Schneier explain in the MIT Technology Review.[61]

This quote stood out to me for two reasons: first, were the lessons around social media actually learned? Second, if hindsight is 20/20 then what might our future sight be if we applied relevant historical context? The article's title is, "Let's Not Make the Same Mistakes with AI That We Made With Social Media." There were many items in the article that really stood out to me. One of the most compelling, which is also the most alarming, was the following statement, "The risks that AI poses to society are strikingly familiar, but there is one big difference: it's not too late. This time, we know it's all coming. Fresh off our experience with the harms wrought by social media, we have all the warning we should need to avoid the same mistakes." This thought-provoking quote offers a comprehensive historical analysis and a stark warning about the consequences of allowing emerging technologies to develop without proper regulation. Moreover, it encourages us to deeply reflect on the idea that even with agreeable guidelines in place, AI's potential to solve problems and create more equitable learning opportunities requires thorough analytical consideration.

Consider the following reflection questions: How have we benefited from social media? How has social media harmed society? Here's the thing, we can easily point to both given how prevalent the impact social media has had and continues to have on our society. But while hindsight can be 20/20 foresight can also be 20/20. What are the questions we should be asking about AI? What are the guiding principles we should demand from developers using this technology based on their intended impact in education? I am reminded of a quote from Don Norman, "A brilliant solution to the wrong problem can be worse than no solution at all; solve the correct problem."[62] A careful examination of past practices reveals a troubling trend in education: the development and design of solutions often precede a thorough understanding of the problems they intend to address. This approach, which can be likened to the idiom "wag the dog," involves searching for problems to justify the implementation of a pre-determined solution.

I generally like to describe this in the following metaphor, "it's a hammer looking for a nail." How often in education are solutions presented for problems that don't exist? Just as bad is the focus on the symptom and not the disease. In order for true equitable solutions to be within our grasp, it is *vital that we confront the actual problems that exist and look to AI as part of the solution. Overlooking this now leads us down the road of predictability; and, if it's predictable it's also preventable. Otherwise, we will likely end up reading articles like that ten years from now performing a type of tech autopsy attempting to figure out what went wrong, which is likely going to be due to not listening to the right voices in the present.*

Challenging the Status Quo: Addressing AI Harms

The core question persists: How is AI currently being utilized in education, and does this utilization merely perpetuate longstanding inequities and dysfunctions? Some have suggested AI's potential to enhance efficiency, but given the ongoing harm inflicted on marginalized student groups, there are fears it could accelerate these destructive patterns. Yet here lies an opportunity. While not obvious, AI presents a chance to defy the status quo and catalyze significant, positive change in education. By thoughtfully leveraging these tools, teachers and students alike could implement genuinely innovative practices that break free from stale conventional approaches. We aim to conclude this book with highlights from previous chapters and reflections on how to move forward in elevating ethics and equity in the conversation of AI use in education.

A recent observation highlights the concerning state of education—children today often proceed through nearly identical processes as past generations. AI implementation has largely remixed existing practices, simply increasing the speed of implementation. Assessments have progressed from manual grading to scantrons to online forms, but multiple-choice testing itself remains unchallenged. AI now offers faster grading automation, but is this truly progressive if the underlying assessment structure is flawed? Clearly, a reconsideration of our approaches is needed. The repetitive cycle of multiple-choice tests and formulaic writing assignments is becoming stale, if not actively harmful. As many educators recognize, we are overdue for a pedagogical breakthrough—an opportunity to boldly implement different strategies that move beyond rote skills toward authentic, engaged learning.

The late Maya Angelou's words ring powerfully true: "Courage is the most important of all the virtues because without courage, you can't practice any other virtue consistently." To challenge education's status quo with AI demands bravery—the courage to self-reflect, self-interrogate, innovate, and step outside the norm. At its core, this shift requires personal and personable courage—a values-driven commitment to using AI as a catalyst for dismantling systemic barriers and empowering marginalized students, not just optimizing for administrative convenience. It necessitates diligent self-examination: What elements of the status quo are we perpetuating, perhaps unintentionally? How can we leverage AI as a transformative force for equity?

To begin defying the status quo, we are called upon to boldly identify actions demonstrating this ethos of courageous change. Dismantling generational inequities using emerging technologies like AI is a prime example. When confronted with the predictability of outcomes for certain student groups, we can no longer accept inaction.

Actively disrupting these cycles is an act of moral courage. This process hinges on awareness—without it, an unintentional and passive perseverance of the status quo is the default. Thoughtful commitment precedes knowing the exact path forward. It means championing critical pedagogy by challenging norms, questioning practices, and striving to actualize a more empowering, authentic model of learning. It means embracing project-based learning that incorporates students' backgrounds and lived experiences. Imagine a history class where students research and present on historical figures or events significant to their own cultural heritage. AI can play a supportive role here. For example, an AI-powered research assistant could be used to curate culturally diverse source materials in multiple languages. This would empower students to delve deeper into their chosen topics while simultaneously fostering critical thinking skills as they evaluate the information presented. This integration of AI complements the culturally relevant curriculum, enhancing the learning experience without overshadowing the core focus on student identity and heritage.

What if we revolutionized teaching by making it a dialogue, not a lecture? What if we rebelled against the antiquated "banking" model of depositing information for regurgitation? In a concept called the forgetting curve, research shows 90 percent of this content is forgotten within two weeks, even among high scorers—a clear indictment of perpetuating this broken system.[63] Instead of using AI for repetitive tasks like generating worksheets or simple multiple-choice questions, we can leverage its potential to evolve and create entirely new possibilities in education. It is important to note here that using technology to recreate or remix low efficacy learning opportunities does not create new possibilities. It simply replicates the same results just through a different means. Design thinking methods could help prototype creative new approaches, and AI itself could augment our ideation around more equitable and effective models. No matter the method you prefer—whether it's Liberatory Design[64], Solve in Time![65] or others—the iterative process of design thinking allows educators and designers to experiment with different approaches and ensure the final solution is truly culturally relevant and meets the needs of diverse learners. The AI element becomes a collaborative partner in the learning process, enhancing the educational experience without overshadowing the importance of cultural identity.[66]

Consider this scenario: An educator enters a learning space believing that learners are empty vessels awaiting knowledge. The plan is to assess students based on how well they memorize and regurgitate information. From a critical pedagogy perspective, this approach creates a potentially harmful power dynamic. By assuming the position of ultimate knowledge source, the educator undermines the learning process and ignores the potential contributions of learners. This traditional approach fails to acknowledge the value of students' experiences and insights. It grants educators undue power, positioning them as the sole arbiters of knowledge. AI can be leveraged to challenge these dynamics, fostering a more equitable learning environment and promoting a more effective educational experience. Resistance to the responsible use of AI in education may stem from its potential to disrupt traditional power structures. A similar resistance arose with the introduction of Google search in classrooms. The argument was that students would simply find answers without true learning. However, this argument misses two crucial points. First, if answers are easily found, perhaps educators should ask more complex questions. Second, this resistance suggests a prioritization of information regurgitation over developing information literacy skills—the ability to use emerging technologies to find and evaluate information.

AI offers an opportunity to rethink these dynamics. In providing student writing feedback, for instance, educators can maintain a power structure where they are the sole feedback source, or they can offer students options, including AI tools. This latter approach empowers students and encourages ownership of their learning process. This empowerment connects to the concept of **culturally responsive education**, which necessitates an awareness of power dynamics and active efforts to dismantle those that reward dominance. Culturally responsive educators recognize and challenge these dynamics, creating a more equitable and productive learning environment.

This experience challenges the idea that AI is solely used for "cheating." Effective AI use still demands higher-order thinking. Users must skillfully frame prompts to get the most useful responses, a process requiring critical analysis and deep subject knowledge. AI, therefore, can be a powerful tool for enhancing learning. To illustrate, consider the prompt: "Take on the role and perspective of an experienced high school teacher who implements critical pedagogy with your students. Apply critical theory to address AI problems in schools. Include examples that can foster in class discussions, critical thinking, and analytical thinking. The discussions are to occur in a class of 11th grade students."

The AI tool used at the time suggested a series of strategies to develop critical consciousness, including:

- Challenge Power Dynamics: Uncover and dismantle unequal power structures within educational systems.
- Expose Hidden Biases: Unmask underlying assumptions and biases potentially embedded in AI tools and educational materials.
- Scrutinize Corporate Interests: Critically analyze the motivations and goals behind corporations promoting AI in education.
- Investigate Objectively: Test claims about AI with neutrality and a discerning eye.
- Uncover Data Issues: Research data ownership, potential biases, and the algorithms that drive AI systems.
- Examine Access and Equity: Investigate issues of unequal access to technology and potential for surveillance within AI-powered education.
- Empower Collective Action: Work together to advocate for ethical and equitable uses of AI in education.

These suggestions reveal AI's educational potential. However, implementing them effectively demands a deep understanding of critical pedagogy. Those unfamiliar with this approach might find the strategies overwhelming. Despite this, the suggestions offer a roadmap for leveraging AI to enhance teaching and create more equitable learning environments. They demonstrate AI's potential as a tool for promoting critical thinking, challenging power dynamics, and fostering a deeper understanding of the world.

Yet enacting this vision requires understanding how AI operates. Students must gain prompt engineering skills to generate relevant, productive AI outputs instead of random responses. They need fluency in providing contextual information—a core principle for mitigating AI risks like bias or harmful content. In fact, developing digital literacies around AI functionality, strengths, and limitations should be a key educational focus. Critical analysis abilities like scrutinizing data sources, examining potential biases and so-called blind spots, and discerning appropriate AI use cases, all empower learners as discerning citizens in an AI-driven world.

Students must be equipped with the investigative skills for ethical engagement with AI around power dynamics, privilege, and marginalization. Which voices are represented in AI training data, and whose are excluded? Are these tools used primarily for profit, or can they serve genuine learning goals and promote equity? Rather than regurgitating answers, effective AI integration involves learning to persistently ask nuanced, probing questions: How might bias manifest in this language model's outputs? How could differential access to AI resources exacerbate digital divides? What accountability structures and protocols govern this system's development and deployment?

This journey is a constant dance—a continuous cycle of inquiry, reflection, and refinement as AI capabilities and societal implications evolve. A fixed approach clashes with the goal of building an authentically empowering, equitable model. We have to remain vigilant, grounding AI usage in timeless pedagogical principles while embracing continuous learning alongside technological advancements. AI can be more than a shortcut; it's a thought partner helping us deepen our understanding through questioning. The goal is empowering both educators and learners to wield AI as a catalyst for developing critical consciousness around power, privilege, and transformative change.

Principles for Practice: Reducing Risks and Bias

Integrating AI responsibly demands upholding key principles around equity, empowerment, transparency and ethics. Cultivating digital and data literacies empowers students and educators alike to leverage AI effectively while equipping them to analyze outputs, identify biases, and provide vital context to mitigate harmful outputs. Crucially, ethical AI goes beyond technical mastery—it necessitates a holistic commitment to learner agency, diverse representation, and equitable outcomes. The aim is to empower customized, inclusive learning pathways driven by student voices and experiences. This approach counters merely automating conventional practices or prioritizing administrator convenience over true pedagogical innovation.

An ethical integration plan centers on bridging the digital divide by ensuring robust access to tools and countering systemic barriers that disproportionately deter minoritized students from STEM career pathways. It elevates the often-marginalized voices of learners, families, and community partners through sustained dialogue and co-creation to ensure AI implementations reflect collective needs. At its best, AI can be a democratizing force—expanding educational opportunity, giving voice to the underrepresented, and equipping all students with future-proof skills. However, this potential hinges on upholding social awareness as a core principle, not just technical acumen. For instance, AI writing assistants trained on datasets representing diverse cultures can be truly empowering tools for multilingual learners.

Yet embracing AI shouldn't come at the expense of skilled human educators and the irreplaceable bonds they forge with students. No AI system can ever fully replicate a caring teacher's ability to nurture the whole child, adapt to individual needs, and make complex judgments that require emotional intelligence. The true power lies in harnessing technology and human strengths synergistically to create equitable learning experiences. This balanced vision requires us to continuously re-evaluate core pedagogical questions. Does a given AI tool genuinely enhance outcomes for all students? Are there potential risks of misuse, bias, or other harms without proper safeguards in place? And most importantly, does this technology authentically personalize learning and amplify diverse perspectives within the classroom?

Building upon this synergistic approach, we recognize that responsible AI integration is an iterative process, not a static implementation. As technologies evolve, so must our policies, training approaches, and oversight mechanisms. We have a duty to remain open to revisiting assumptions, fostering transparency around AI systems, elevating marginalized stakeholder voices, and adapting practices based on new insights. The aim is nurturing adaptable learning communities centered on continuous improvement through open collaboration. Schools should become innovation hubs where educators, students, families, and community partners co-create and rigorously evaluate AI integration in service of humanistic, equitable education principles.

Fundamentally, the path forward harmonizes new technologies with timeless ethical wisdom. It's guided by beacons of equity, empowerment, inclusion, courage, creativity, and an unwavering commitment to learner agency. It requires centering student voices, fostering community partnerships, and embracing a spirit of iterative co-creation. By upholding these ideals, schools can become springboards actualizing each learner's full potential in an AI-driven world—not conformity factories perpetuating the entrenched inequities of an outdated model.

Taking Action: The Role of Activism

Dr. Angelou's statement about courage being the pinnacle of virtues is especially true when we consider utilizing AI to disrupt the predictability of education outcomes. This is truly a revolutionary act. To fight against the system, to oppose the status quo, and to consider using technology to revamp the system we all thought would be transformed post-pandemic will not go without opposition. In addition to challenging, you to think differently about AI in education, we have a deep desire for you to become changemakers. To act revolutionarily. To transform education as we know it. The true power of AI in education lies in its potential to unlock equity and empower learners. But lofty ideals won't translate to reality without courageous and sustained action. It is our responsibility to move beyond theoretical discussions and actively challenge the status quo. This is the promise of AI use we are most excited about.

This means holding corporations accountable for biased products, advocating for policies and funding that prioritize ethical AI integration, and prioritizing learner-centered innovation over administrative convenience. Within classrooms, fostering an environment where students champion AI ethics is crucial. By engaging in participatory action research, young people can see firsthand how algorithmic bias plays out in their communities. Armed with this knowledge, they can become powerful advocates for transparency in AI development and demand a more inclusive voice in shaping technology decisions. Outside of schools, community partners, families, and grassroots organizers play an indispensable role shaping an equitable AI future. By elevating overlooked issues, uplifting marginalized voices, and mobilizing collective pressure, their moral authority and lived experiences demand AI be deployed as a tool of justice, not oppression.

Educators hold a critical role in shaping the future of AI in education. To ensure these tools benefit all students, they must cultivate a commitment to lifelong learning, continuously seeking new ways to leverage AI in ways that are both socially responsible and demonstrably effective for diverse learners. This requires a multifaceted approach. First, educators must acknowledge their own inherent biases to minimize their influence on AI implementation. Second, they should actively advocate for diverse representation within AI development and implementation teams. This ensures the tools themselves reflect the rich tapestry of human experience and avoids perpetuating existing biases. Finally, educators must develop a habit of constantly re-evaluating classroom AI tools through an equity lens, remaining vigilant in identifying potential biases and their impact on student learning.

The path forward demands a collective effort. By raising our voices in unison, united by moral courage, we can rewrite the narrative surrounding AI in education. Through sustained activism, deep partnerships, educators and stakeholders can collaborate to ensure AI becomes a catalyst for pedagogical revolutions. This collective effort will dismantle educational inequities, not entrench them further, and pave the way for a brighter future where AI empowers all learners. Our shared actions today will determine whether these technologies become instruments of freedom or oppression in the classrooms of tomorrow. We need to see ourselves as empowered protagonists co-authoring AI's unfolding story in the service of educational justice.

A core aspect of this work is defending students' agency to critically analyze and reshape AI's impacts themselves. The classroom must be re-envisioned as an empowering space for inquiry, critique, and co-construction—not passive content consumption. Students should lead participatory action research unpacking AI biases across communities, using findings to drive policy reforms and corporate accountability campaigns. Likewise, design thinking projects could engage learners in prototyping AI systems embodying values like transparency and fairness by design. Young people can leverage communication platforms to amplify marginalized voices, share counterstories highlighting those harmed by unethical AI, and launch creative social movements demanding change. This activism nurtures digital literacies while developing the socially conscious mindsets needed to ethically steward transformative technologies.

However, realizing this vision requires a paradigm shift. Students can no longer be positioned as recipients of AI tools disproportionately benefiting corporate interests and privileged groups. They must become empowered investigators and activists dismantling injustice coded into these powerful systems. Cultivating this spirit of critical consciousness and civic agency should be a core aim of AI-integrated education models. Additionally, activism around ethical AI integration must extend beyond the classroom. Each of us must engage in the difficult but crucial work of self-reflection to understand how our assumptions and positionality influence our ability to be responsible stewards of these technologies. Humility is essential—recognizing that even with the best intentions, our existing mental models likely suffer from limitations. We have an obligation to create spaces for marginalized voices to expand our awareness around issues like AI bias, data inequities, and flawed accountability structures. Only by grounding AI decisions in community wisdom can we act from a place of true integrity.

In the end, the story of education AI remains very much unfinished and unwritten. Its narrative arc is not predetermined by the tools themselves, but by the collective vision we bring to bear in their development and implementation. Through student empowerment, community partnership, and activist mindsets, we can steer AI as a force for dismantling inequity and catalyzing humanistic, learner-driven educational transformation. Conversely, if we remain passive and closed off to critical dialogue, these technologies risk exacerbating injustice under the guise of innovation. AI's potential tomorrows are being shaped by our moral actions today. We cannot idly wait for an ethical future to spontaneously emerge—we have an ethical responsibility to actively demand and manifest the realities we wish to see. Constructing an equitable AI-integrated educational model will be an uphill battle against entrenched systemic forces. We face obstacles like bureaucratic inertia, lack of funding for ethical AI research and development, misaligned corporate incentives that profit from biased status quo systems, and more.[67]

Yet even in the face of such daunting challenges, relinquishing an activist's conviction cedes power and grants tacit permission for injustice to persist. When opportunities arise to bend technology's arc toward liberation, complacency becomes complicity with oppression. The stakes are simply too high—the potential for AI to shape the future of entire generations hangs in the balance. Paralysis in the face of difficulty cannot be an option. This transformation requires a collective effort across the entire educational ecosystem. Policymakers need to feel the pressure to enact legislation that incentivizes ethical AI use and empowers communities to hold corporations accountable. Technology companies must be pushed to open their AI development processes to public oversight and embrace inclusive co-design practices. Funding mechanisms that prioritize rapid automation at the expense of quality, equitable learning must be fundamentally overhauled.

At the ground level, a different kind of education is needed. Students, families, and educators all require training in AI ethics, the societal impacts of these technologies, and the critical skills needed to navigate the world of data—data literacy. Through sustained advocacy, policy reforms, community-building, and grassroots empowerment, we can reshape educational AI's trajectory in service of profound human priorities—human potential, agency, and flourishing.

However, anchoring our activism in hope is paramount. We also must have faith that when guided by diverse, empowered stakeholders, AI can illuminate solutions to systemic injustice rather than obfuscating it. That these technologies' evolution can bend society's arc closer to our highest ideals of equity, inclusion and human thriving. Yet this hope must be balanced by a humble recognition—the path toward ethical integration will be iterative, labyrinthine, and require constant re-evaluation. It is necessary for us to accept missteps as inevitable, using them as crucibles for deeper understanding and recommitting to courageous course-corrections.

Creating an open culture where difficult, and necessary, conversations around AI's limitations, risks, and harms are encouraged rather than avoided is critical. For too long, those who benefited from unequal systems have had the privilege of ignoring hard truths. If we seek authentic progress, this selective ignorance is untenable. Likewise, transparency and truth-telling around AI's genuine current capabilities is foundational. It is vital we resist sweeping utopian or dystopian narratives, insisting instead on clear-eyed assessments anchored in present-day realities. Only through such honest reckoning can we begin charting a reasoned, ethical path forward. At each turn, it becomes even more necessary that we insist on elevating diverse rightsholder voices—students, families, community groups, and educators across contexts. Their moral authority, first-hand experiences, and brilliant insights prevent our work from becoming esoteric thought exercises irrelevant to those most impacted. Equity work divorced from equitable process is self-undermining.

This humble but hopeful process of transparent, inclusive, ongoing collaboration to integrate AI ethically will not be easy. Yet difficulty is no excuse for inaction or resignation, for we are shapers of these technologies, not merely passive recipients. With community as our pilots and justice as our compass, the long arc of progress can bend towards empowering classrooms where AI enables human flourishing, not its erosion. Our shared activism must carry this vision forward. The journey of AI in education has only just begun. Within these pages, we've explored both the potential and the pitfalls of integrating these powerful tools into classrooms. The path forward hinges not on technology itself, but on the collective vision we bring to bear in wielding it.

By empowering students, fostering community partnerships, and embracing an activist mindset, we can ensure AI serves as a force for equity and justice. Classrooms can become crucibles for forging a future where technology amplifies human potential, not diminishes it. Let us not be passive bystanders in this unfolding narrative. Let us pick up the pen, raise our voices, and co-author a story where AI illuminates pathways to a brighter, more just educational landscape for all.

Conclusion

DL:

*Maybe you looked past it, but on the very first page of this book, we provided a disclaimer about how this book was formulated. It started as a series of recorded phone conversations based on the outline we prepared in advance. Per usual, we had our notes and intended talking points, but then the conversation led us down different paths as we played off one another's thoughts, experiences, and education. That's how a conversation with my brother Ken goes. Sometimes he mentions points that leave me simply nodding my head and adding nothing but an affirming "yup!" Sometimes it's like double Dutch—either of us listening intently for a place where it makes sense to mention something we've prepared to share. Other times, a point is made that conjures up a completely different thought, and a planned 30-minute conversation extends to 90-minutes plus. This is how we collaborate and complement one another. Further, we used AI tools to help reapply our signature **CPT** segments, transcribe our conversations, and transform our dialogue into a cohesive written voice. Then the writing, rewriting, and editing began.*

We also used AI and grammar-editing tools to correct our grammatical errors and rearrange our points for better consistency and flow. We then went back into the text and made manual edits, added more research and anecdotes, and even wove in a few additional individual stories like the one you are reading now. We also hired a proofreader and copy editor to help us shore up our writing even more. What we believe we have created is a working example of how AI can be used effectively without compromising ethical use. Our transparency in its use and our critical thoughts concerning ways it can potentially create harm have been our attempt to elevate equity. Notice we have NOT highlighted the use of AI as a way to increase efficiency. If AI could have made this work more efficient, then it would have been published several months earlier! Further, the quality would likely have decreased dramatically. Principally, efficiency is not just the enemy of quality; it is the enemy of equity. Efficiency and greed are what have created the wealth and technology gaps that exist between classes— both social structures and rooms filled with students (read that bar again).

Maybe you disagree with this assessment, which is absolutely your right to do so. We hope you spend time rereading this book, continuing to fill in the margins with your noticings and wonderings. We look forward to your mentions on social media and face-to-face dialogue at conferences and workshops. Whatever your opinion, get your research ready because, just like generative AI, the advancements and complexity of the conversation continue.

Like many other books, Ken and I didn't finalize the title or cover art until most of the text was complete. Only after considering everything, we'd produced did we start deliberating on the title that best captures the essence of the book and the imagery that would most accurately represent it. I am very interested in your analysis of the cover art. I'm curious how you will integrate your personal experiences and viewpoints to reach your own conclusions. Here's my brief interpretation:

The left side of the cover represents **Afrofuturism**, while the right side suggests the possibility of Afro-extinction. Here's what I mean: if you've seen either Black Panther movie or are a fan of the MCU in general, like Ken and me, you can't help but marvel at Shuri's scientific and technological genius or the analytical power of the AI assistant, Griot (fun fact: voiced by Trevor Noah). The promise of humans harnessing technology for humanity's survival and overall quality of life is something we all imagine, and for which we've invested our dollars and data.

But on the other side lies a more daunting thought: What if robots really do take over? What if we lose our humanity altogether? Even more terrifying, what if the future of technology isn't simply integration but complete annihilation, particularly of the identity, freedom, and beauty of Black and Brown people? The only way to prevent the latter, I believe, is to develop and utilize AI differently, starting in educational institutions. This is our call to action, our commitment, because our very existence is on the line.

KS:

As we conclude this book, I am left with feelings of both optimism and guarded cynicism. Artificial intelligence is being looked at as a "disruptor" in many circles. The problem I have with this is true disruption is temporary. What lessons should we have learned and taken forward with us after March 13, 2020? If anything, the pandemic exposed to many what those of us whose voices are often relegated to the *margins have been saying for decades now. Our digital resources are not equitably distributed, broadband internet access is still not ubiquitous, learning environments that may be digital-resource rich can simultaneously be pedagogy-poor, and education as a whole still remains absurdly under supported in tangible ways.*

When I look at some schools or school systems, I see an often-predictable dynamic that we examined in several chapters here—if a school or system is under-resourced then mathematically there are schools and systems that are over-resourced. The optimism around artificial intelligence I hold is that it just might give us the opportunity to address this disparity. It might hold the promise that we are looking to see operationalized within all of our learning environments. AI is not the panacea to the disparity problem; rather, it is one of many essential components that must be in place, alongside broadband internet access, a device-agnostic approach, relevant, authentic, and responsive teaching and learning, the meaningful and transformative use of technology, and the provision of necessary support to all members of the education community to build momentum for change.

But as we have laid out in this book, that needs to occur both strategically and diligently. It is imperative that we remain vigilant in how we approach our understanding and usage of artificial intelligence, especially the platforms propagated and promoted within education. I am often reminded of a quote I like to share from the late Coach John Wooden, "Be quick but don't hurry."[68] Let's be quick to learn and understand, but don't hurry where our haste becomes yet another learning trap.

Glossary

Afrofuturism: A cultural aesthetic and philosophy that explores the intersection of African diaspora culture with science, technology, and futurism. It envisions empowering futures for Black people through the creative use of technology and science fiction.

Algorithmic auditing: The process of assessing and evaluating algorithms, including those used in AI systems, to identify and mitigate potential biases, errors, or unintended consequences. Algorithmic auditing involves examining the data, logic, and outcomes of algorithmic decision-making to ensure transparency, fairness, and accountability. In the context of AI and education, algorithmic auditing is an essential tool for uncovering and addressing biases that may be embedded in AI-powered educational technologies, such as adaptive learning platforms or predictive analytics tools.

Algorithmic bias: The systematic and unfair discrimination in AI algorithms due to biases in the training data or the design of the algorithms themselves, leading to unequal treatment of different groups based on characteristics like race, gender, or socioeconomic status.

Application Program Interface (API): A set of protocols, routines, and tools for building software applications, which specifies how software components should interact.

Artificial intelligence (AI): The simulation of human intelligence in machines that are programmed to think, learn, and adapt. AI systems can perform tasks that typically require human intelligence, such as visual perception, speech recognition, decision-making, and language translation.

Bandwagon effect: A cognitive bias that occurs when people adopt beliefs or behaviors because many other people are doing the same, often without critically examining the merits of those beliefs or behaviors.

Black boxes: Opaque or non-transparent AI systems whose inner workings are not easily understood or interpretable. Black box AI models, particularly complex deep learning models, can be difficult to explain or audit, making it challenging to identify biases, errors, or unintended consequences in their decision-making processes. The lack of transparency in black box AI systems raises concerns about accountability, fairness, and trust, especially in high-stakes applications like education, where decisions can significantly impact students' lives.

Chatbot: An AI program designed to simulate conversation with human users, often used for customer service, information retrieval, and personal assistants.

ChatGPT: A generative AI model developed by OpenAI that uses natural language processing to generate human-like text based on user inputs. It gained rapid popularity due to its ability to produce coherent and contextually relevant content.

Choice-supportive bias: The tendency to retroactively ascribe positive attributes to the option one has selected, and to demote the forgone options.

Conflict theory: A sociological perspective that views society as an arena of inequality that generates conflict and change. It highlights the power struggles between different social groups, such as the "haves" and "have-nots."

Children's Online Privacy Protection Act (COPPA): A US federal law that regulates the online collection of personal information from children under the age of 13. COPPA imposes requirements on website and online service operators to provide notice and obtain verifiable parental consent before collecting personal information from children. It aims to protect children's privacy and give parents control over what information is collected from their kids online. As educational technology and AI applications involve collecting data from students, COPPA compliance is an important consideration.

Community reading experience: The phenomenon of a piece of content, such as a video, image, article, or social media post, being widely shared and consumed within a specific online community, often without regard for its accuracy or credibility.

Copium: An internet slang term used to describe the act of clinging to unfounded optimism or denial in the face of disappointment or defeat. It's a humorous portmanteau of the words "cope" and "opium," implying that the person is using wishful thinking as a way to numb the pain of reality. For example, after Kendrick Lamar picked Drake's carcass apart, then obliterated him with "Not Like Us", some Drake fans took to social media using copium posting things like "Drake had the better raps, Kendrick just had the most shock value!" For all Kendrick fans, the convincing win was truly euphoric.

Colored People's Time (CPT)- Colored People's Time (CPT) is an expression in the United States that refers to the stereotype of African Americans being frequently late. It implies a relaxed or indifferent attitude towards punctuality, which can lead to negative stereotypes about laziness or unreliability.

It's important to note that this is a stereotype, and punctuality can vary among people regardless of race. There are also social and historical factors that can influence perceptions of timeliness.

Culturally responsive education: A pedagogy that recognizes the importance of including students' cultural references in all aspects of learning and seeks to make learning encounters more relevant to and effective for students from diverse backgrounds.

Datasets: A collection of data that is used to train, test, and evaluate AI systems. Datasets can include various types of data, such as text, images, audio, or numerical data, and are typically organized and labeled in a way that makes them suitable for machine learning tasks. In the context of education, datasets play a crucial role in developing and deploying AI-powered tools and platforms that can personalize learning, assess student performance, and provide targeted support.

Data cleansing: The process of identifying, correcting, or removing inaccurate, incomplete, or irrelevant data from a dataset. Data cleansing is a crucial step in preparing data for use in AI systems, as it helps to ensure the quality, consistency, and reliability of the data used to train and evaluate these systems. In the context of AI and education, data cleansing is particularly important given the sensitive nature of educational data and the potential impact of data-driven decisions on students' lives.

Data literacy: The ability to read, understand, create, and communicate data as information. It includes understanding how to use data effectively and ethically in various contexts.

Data provenance: Information about the origin, history, and chain of custody of data. In the context of AI systems, data provenance refers to tracking the sources, transformations, and movements of the datasets used to train AI models. It helps establish data lineage, ensuring transparency about where the training data came from and how it was processed.

Data weighting: The process of adjusting the importance or influence of certain data points or features in a dataset to account for biases, imbalances, or other factors that may skew the results of an AI system. Data weighting involves assigning different weights or coefficients to individual data points based on their relevance, reliability, or representativeness. In the context of AI and education, data weighting is a technique used to address biases and ensure fairness in AI-powered tools and decision-making processes.

Deep learning: A subset of machine learning that uses algorithms inspired by the structure and function of the brain called artificial neural networks.

Digital divide: The gap between those who have ready access to computers and the internet, and those who do not, due to socioeconomic, geographic, or other factors.

Digital equity: The fair access to digital tools, resources, and opportunities necessary for full participation in society. It involves addressing disparities in technology access and usage among different socioeconomic groups.

Digital literacy: The ability to use information technology and digital media to find, evaluate, create, and share information effectively, responsibly, and safely.

Disinformation: False, inaccurate, or misleading information that is spread deliberately with the intent to deceive or manipulate. In the context of AI, disinformation can be generated and amplified by AI systems, such as chatbots or deepfakes, to influence public opinion, sow confusion, or undermine trust.

Equity: The provision of resources, opportunities, and support tailored to individual or group needs to achieve fair outcomes. In AI contexts, it involves designing systems that recognize and address disparities, ensuring all users benefit equally regardless of their background or circumstances.

Ethical AI: The study and application of moral principles to the development and use of artificial intelligence. It includes considerations of fairness, accountability, transparency, and the potential societal impact of AI technologies. In the context of this book, it asks questions like, "Is it against the law? What if someone did this to me? Am I sacrificing the long-term for a short-term gain?"

European Union's General Data Protection Regulation (GDPR): A comprehensive data protection law that went into effect in 2018, establishing rules for how organizations must handle personal data of individuals within the European Union. The GDPR focuses on principles like data minimization, purpose limitation, storage limitation, integrity and confidentiality, and accountability. It grants individuals rights over their personal data, including the right to access, rectify, erase, and port their data.

Facial recognition technology: A biometric technology that uses algorithms to identify or verify individuals based on their facial features. It is used in various applications, including security and surveillance, but raises concerns about privacy and bias.

Family Educational Rights and Privacy Act (FERPA): A federal law that protects the privacy of student education records. FERPA gives parents certain rights with respect to their children's education records, such as the right to inspect and review those records. It also restricts the disclosure of personally identifiable information from education records without prior written parental consent, with some exceptions. FERPA applies to all schools that receive funds under an applicable program of the US Department of Education. As AI systems in education may handle student data, ensuring FERPA compliance is crucial for protecting student privacy.

Gartner hype cycle: A graphical representation developed by Gartner—a research, advisory, and information technology company—that describes the maturity, adoption, and social application of emerging technologies. The cycle consists of five phases: Innovation Trigger, Peak of Inflated Expectations, Trough of Disillusionment, Slope of Enlightenment, and Plateau of Productivity. In the context of AI and education, the Gartner hype cycle can help educators, administrators, and policymakers understand the current state of AI technologies, set realistic expectations, and make informed decisions about their adoption and implementation in educational settings.

Generative AI: A type of artificial intelligence that can create new content, such as text, images, and music, by learning from existing data. Examples include ChatGPT and DALL-E, which can generate human-like text and images, respectively.

Hallucination: When an AI system confidently generates false or nonsensical output that appears convincing or plausible at first glance.

Inclusion: The practice or policy of providing equal access to opportunities and resources for people who might otherwise be excluded or marginalized.

Justice: In the context of AI and equity, iustice refers to the fair and unbiased application of AI systems and algorithms. It ensures that these technologies do not perpetuate or exacerbate existing societal inequalities based on factors like race, gender, or socioeconomic status.

Large language models (LLMs): AI models trained on vast amounts of text data to understand and generate human language. These models can perform a variety of language tasks, including translation, summarization, and conversation.

Machine learning (ML): A subset of AI that involves training algorithms on large datasets to enable them to make predictions or decisions without being explicitly programmed to perform specific tasks.

Malinformation: Accurate information that is shared with the intent to cause harm, often by taking it out of context or using it to promote a particular agenda. In the context of AI, malinformation can occur when AI systems are used to selectively present or manipulate data in ways that are misleading or damaging, such as reinforcing stereotypes or undermining educational goals.

Marginalization: Treatment of a person, group, or concept as insignificant or peripheral.

Media literacy: The ability to access, analyze, evaluate, create, and act using all forms of communication. In the context of AI and education, media literacy involves understanding how AI-generated content is created, distributed, and consumed, as well as developing the skills to critically evaluate and responsibly use AI technologies.

Misinformation: False, inaccurate, or misleading information that is spread unintentionally. In the context of AI, misinformation can arise from AI-generated content that is biased, inconsistent, or lacking proper context.

Natural language processing (NLP): A field of AI focused on the interaction between computers and humans through natural language. NLP enables machines to understand, interpret, and generate human language.

Neural networks: A type of machine learning algorithm that is modeled after the structure and function of the human brain. Neural networks consist of interconnected nodes, or "neurons," that process and transmit information in a way that allows the system to learn and adapt based on input data. In the context of AI and education, neural networks are used to power a wide range of applications, such as personalized learning platforms, adaptive assessments, and intelligent tutoring systems. These networks can learn to recognize patterns, make predictions, and generate new content based on vast amounts of educational data.

Personalized learning: An educational approach that tailor's instruction to the individual needs, strengths, and interests of each student. AI can facilitate personalized learning by providing adaptive feedback and customized learning experiences.

Personally identifiable information (PII): Data that can be used to identify a specific individual. This includes obvious identifiers like names, social security numbers, and addresses, as well as less obvious pieces of information like biometric data (fingerprints, facial images, etc.), IP addresses, geolocation data, or unique identifiers across different systems. In the context of education, protecting PII is crucial to ensuring student privacy and security, as AI systems often rely on vast amounts of personal data to provide personalized and adaptive learning experiences.

Plagiarism: The act of using someone else's work, ideas, or intellectual property without proper attribution, presenting it as one's own. In the context of AI, it refers to concerns about students using AI-generated content without acknowledgment. Educators and institutions must develop policies and guidelines to address the ethical implications of using AI tools in academic work and to promote academic integrity in the age of AI.

Pluralism: A philosophical and social concept that recognizes and values diversity in cultures, beliefs, and practices within a society. In the context of AI, pluralism emphasizes the importance of developing and deploying AI systems that are inclusive, equitable, and respectful of the diverse needs and perspectives of learners and educators.

Prompt engineering: The process of designing effective prompts to elicit desired outputs from AI systems. Exemplified in this book is using the basic prompt formula of giving the LLM a personality or perspective, a purpose, and parameters. After a response is given, then continue to polish the results by adding parameters or clarification i.e. practice, refine, practice, refine.

Protection of Pupil Rights Amendment: A federal law in the US that affords certain rights to parents and students regarding surveys, evaluations, and other materials that may collect sensitive personal information from students. The PPRA requires that schools and contractors obtain parental consent before administering certain types of surveys or evaluations funded by the US Department of Education, and it allows parents to inspect these materials upon request. In the context of AI, the PPRA is an important safeguard for protecting student privacy and ensuring transparency in the use of educational data. As AI systems increasingly rely on student data to provide personalized learning experiences and inform educational decision-making, compliance with the PPRA helps to ensure that this data is being collected and used in a manner that respects students' and parents' rights and promotes trust in the educational system.

Rightsholder: A term preferred over "stakeholder" to emphasize the inherent rights and legal entitlements of individuals or groups, rather than treating them as mere interested parties. It counters the colonial connotations of "stakeholder" that disregarded indigenous rights and affirms the fundamental human rights of rightsholders like the right to education, privacy, land, and culture.

School-to-prison pipeline: The disproportionate tendency of minors and young adults from disadvantaged backgrounds to become incarcerated because of increasingly harsh school and municipal policies.

Socioeconomic status (SES): The social standing or class of an individual or group, often measured as a combination of education, income, and occupation. SES affects access to resources and opportunities, including technology and education.

Solve In Time!: An educational activity developed by Dee Lanier that uses design thinking principles to guide students through real-world problem-solving.

Synthetic media: Synthetic media refers to artificially generated or manipulated digital content, such as images, videos, audio recordings, or text, created using techniques like deep learning and computer vision. It includes deepfakes, which are highly realistic and almost undetectable videos or images that depict events, actions, or words that never actually occurred. In the context of AI and education, synthetic media raises concerns about the spread of disinformation, plagiarism, and the potential misuse of AI-generated content.

The talk: Refers to the conversations many Black parents have with their children, especially sons, about how to behave and respond if they encounter racism or racial profiling from authorities. It is an unfortunate reality that many Black families in the US feel the need to provide this guidance due to the long history of racism, discrimination, and disproportionately higher policing of Black communities.

Transparency in AI: The practice of making the processes, data, and algorithms used in AI systems open and understandable to users. Transparency helps build trust and allows for the identification and correction of biases and errors.

Unconscious bias: Social stereotypes about certain groups of people that individuals form outside their conscious awareness. In technology, unconscious bias can influence the development and deployment of AI systems, leading to biased outcomes.

Endnotes

Introduction

1. *Killed by Google* - "Killed by Google." Killed by Google, killedbygoogle.com

2. *James Baldwin Speech* - Baldwin, James. "A Talk to Teachers." Speech, 16 Oct. 1963. STS Infrastructures, stsinfrastructures.org/content/baldwin-1963-talk-teachers.

Chapter 1

3. *ChatGPT User Milestone* - Ghosh, Shubham. "ChatGPT hit 1 million users in 5 days: Here's how long it took others to reach that milestone." The Indian Express, 12 Apr. 2024, indianexpress.com/article/technology/artificial-intelligence/chatgpt-hit-1-million-users-5-days-vs-netflix-facebook-instagram-spotify-mark-8394119/.

4. *AI Chatbots and Cheating* - "What Do AI Chatbots Really Mean for Students and Cheating?" Stanford Graduate School of Education, 29 Mar. 2024, ed.stanford.edu/news/what-do-ai-chatbots-really-mean-students-and-cheating.

5. *Social Conflict Theory* - Coser, Lewis A. The Functions of Social Conflict. Free Press, 1956.

6. *Intelligent Tutoring Systems* - Srivastava, Shashank, et al. "Harnessing the Power of AI to Create Intelligent Tutoring Systems for Enhanced Classroom Experience and Improved Learning Outcomes." Intelligent Tutoring

Systems for Enhancing E-Learning, edited by Sanjay K. Dhurandher et al., Springer, 2023, pp. 487-500

7. *Business Textbook* - Brown, Betty J., and John E. Clow. Introduction to Business: Student Edition. 5th ed., McGraw-Hill Education, 2002

8. *AI Text Classifier* - "New AI Classifier for Indicating AI-Written Text." OpenAI, 31 Jan. 2023, openai.com/index/new-ai-classifier-for-indicating-ai-written-text/

9. *Turnitin AI Detector Guidance* - "Guidance on AI Detection and Why We're Disabling Turnitin's AI Detector." Vanderbilt Brightspace Blog, 16 Aug. 2023, www.vanderbilt.edu/brightspace/2023/08/16/guidance-on-ai-detection-and-why-were-disabling-turnitins-ai-detector/

10. *Adapting Classes for AI* - "Adapting Classes to the Artificial Intelligence Era." Center for Teaching Excellence, University of Kansas, 24 Apr. 2024, cte.ku.edu/adapting-classes-artificial-intelligence-era

11. *AI Detector Bias* - "AI-Detectors Biased Against Non-Native English Writers." Stanford Institute for Human-Centered Artificial Intelligence, 29 Mar. 2024, hai.stanford.edu/news/ai-detectors-biased-against-non-native-english-writers

12. *Gender Classification Bias* - Buolamwini, Joy, and Timnit Gebru. "Gender Shades: Intersectional Accuracy Disparities in Commercial Gender Classification." Proceedings of Machine Learning Research, vol. 81, 2018, pp. 77-91

13. *Digital Literacy Textbook* - LaGarde, Jennifer, and Darren Hudgins. Developing Digital Detectives: Essential Lessons to Discern Fact from Fiction in the 'Fake News' Era. ISTE, 2018

Chapter 2

14. *School-to-Prison Pipeline* - Sokolower, Jody. "Michelle Alexander on The New Jim Crow and the School-to-Prison Pipeline." Rethinking Schools, vol. 26, no. 2, 2011, rethinkingschools.org/2011/12/20/michelle-alexander-on-the-new-jim-crow-and-the-school-to-prison-pipeline

15. *CROWN Act* - Gould, Elise, and Jori Kandra. "The CROWN Act: A Jewel for Combating Racial Discrimination in the Workplace and Classroom." Economic Policy Institute, 30 Mar. 2024, www.epi.org/publication/crown-act

16. *School-to-Prison Nexus* - West Wind Education Policy. "Understanding the School-to-Prison Nexus." West Wind, 13 Oct. 2023, westwinded.com/blog/understanding-the-school-to-prison-nexus/

17. *Equity in Design* - Lanier, Dee. Demarginalizing Design: Elevating Equity for Real-World Problem Solving. Lanier Learning, 2022

18. *Preschool Expulsion Bias* - Yale News. "Implicit Bias May Explain High Preschool Expulsion Rates for Black Children." Yale News, 27 Sept. 2016, news.yale.edu/2016/09/27/implicit-bias-may-explain-high-preschool-expulsion-rates-black-children

Chapter 3

19. *Pandemic Learning Inequities* - Blume, Howard. "Coronavirus-Caused LAUSD School Shutdown Worsens Inequities as Many Students Go AWOL." Los Angeles Times, 31 Mar. 2020, www.latimes.com/california/story/2020-03-31/coronavirus-school-shutdown-students-awol

20. *Adaptive Learning Platforms* - Whatfix. "7 Best Adaptive Learning Platforms in 2024." Whatfix Blog, 30 Mar. 2024, whatfix.com/blog/adaptive-learning-platforms/

21. *Personalized Learning and AI* - van der Vorst, Tommy, and Nick Jelicic. "Can AI Bring the Full Potential of Personalized Learning to Education?" EconStor, 4 Feb. 2024, www.econstor.eu/bitstream/10419/205222/1/van-der-Vorst-Jelicic.pdf

22. *University AI Access* - Marquette Messenger. "Artificial Intelligence to be Accessible to Students Second Semester." Marquette Messenger, 4 Jan. 2024, marquettemessenger.com/news/2024/01/04/artificial-intelligence-to-be-accessible-to-students-second-semester/

23. *K-12 Generative AI Policy* - Oregon Department of Education. Developing Policy and Protocols for the Use of Generative AI in K-12 Classrooms. Oregon.gov, Feb. 2023, www.oregon.gov/ode/educator-resources/teachingcontent/Documents/ODE_Developing_Policy_and_Protocols_for_the_use_of_Generative_AI_in_K-12_Classrooms_2023.pdf

24. *AI Accessibility* - "Artificial Intelligence for All: How to Make AI Accessible and Inclusive." World Economic Forum, www.weforum.org/agenda/2024/01/artificial-intelligence-ai-innovation-technology-davos-2024/

25. *Engineering Education* - "The Engineer Factory." The Engineer Factory, www.theengineerfactory.org

26. *Community Organization* - Do Greater Charlotte. "Do Greater Charlotte." Do Greater Charlotte, dogreater.org/

27. *UN Sustainable Goal* - "Goal 2: Zero Hunger." United Nations, www.un.org/sustainabledevelopment/hunger/

28. *Science Advisor Appointment* - Subbaraman, Nidhi. "'Inspired choice': Biden appoints sociologist Alondra

Nelson to top science post." NEWS, 21 January 2021, www.nature.com/articles/d41586-021-00159-z

29. *Clean Energy Education* - "Generation 180." Generation 180, generation180.org/our-work.

Chapter 4

30. *Robot Tutor* - "About ABii." Smart Robot Tutor, www.smartrobottutor.com/about-abii

31. *Social Robot* - "Moxie." Moxie, moxierobot.com/v

32. *Robot Racism* - Bartneck, Christoph. "Even Black Robots Are Impacted by Racism." Fast Company, 26 Apr. 2024, www.fastcompany.com/90212508/even-black-robots-are-impacted-by-racism

33. *School Discrimination Study* - Gordon, Rebecca, et al. "Facing the Consequences: An Examination of Racial Discrimination in U.S. Public Schools." ERIC, 2000, eric.ed.gov/?id=ED454323

34. *SAT Bias Correction* - Freedle, R. O. "Correcting the SAT's Ethnic and Social-Class Bias: A Method for Reestimating SAT Scores." Harvard Educational Review, vol. 73, no. 1, 2003, pp. 1-43

35. *Search Engine Bias* - Noble, Safiya Umoja. Algorithms of Oppression: How Search Engines Reinforce Racism. New York University Press, 2018

36. *AI Harm Sources* - Suresh, H., and J. Guttag. "Understanding Potential Sources of Harm throughout the Machine Learning Life Cycle." arXiv, 2021, assets.pubpub.org/k7uu5k6o/c16a07bb-975a-4fec-9c21-102434e277f9.pdf

37. *Algorithmic Bias Book* - O'Neil, Cathy. Weapons of Math Destruction: How Big Data Increases Inequality and Threatens Democracy. Crown Publishers, 2016

38. *Healthcare AI* - Rajkomar, Arjun, et al. "Scalable and Accurate Deep Learning with Electronic Health Records." npj Digital Medicine, vol. 1, no. 1, 2018, pp. 1-10

39. *Affirmative Action Impact* - Cohen, Andrew. "Two Decades Later: Assessing Prop 209's Impact on Legal Education in California." Berkeley Law, 12 Apr. 2024, www.law.berkeley.edu/article/two-decades-later-assessing-prop-209s-impact-on-legal-education-in-california/

40. *Big Data Discrimination* - Barocas, Solon, and Andrew D. Selbst. "Big Data's Disparate Impact." California Law Review, vol. 104, no. 3, 2016, pp. 671-732

41. *AI Bias Blindspot* - Crawford, Kate, and Ryan Calo. "There is a Blind Spot in AI Research." Nature, vol. 538, no. 7625, 2016, pp. 311-313

42. *Algorithmic Bias Book* - O'Neil, Cathy. Weapons of Math Destruction: How Big Data Increases Inequality and Threatens Democracy. Crown Publishers, 2016

43. *Sociotechnical System Fairness* - Selbst, Andrew D., et al. "Fairness and Abstraction in Sociotechnical Systems." ACM FAccT '19: Conference on Fairness, Accountability, and Transparency, 2019, dl.acm.org/doi/10.1145/3287560.3287598

44. *Algorithmic Discrimination Paper* - papers.ssrn.com/sol3/papers.cfm?abstract_id=2376209

45. *Algorithmic Social Contract* - Rahwan, Iyad. "Society-in-the-Loop: Programming the Algorithmic Social Contract." Ethics and Information Technology, vol. 20, no. 1, 2018, pp. 5-14, philpapers.org/rec/RAHSPT

46. *Automated Hiring Audits* - Ajunwa, Ifeoma. "An Auditing Imperative for Automated Hiring Systems." Harvard Journal of Law & Technology, vol. 34, no. 2, 2021, pp. 621-688, jolt.law.harvard.edu/assets/articlePDFs/v34/5.-

Ajunwa-An-Auditing-Imperative-for-Automated-Hiring-Systems.pdf

Chapter 5

47. *Facial Recognition Arrest* - Nicas, Jack. "Facial Recognition Leads to Arrest of Woodbridge Man." The New York Times, 24 June 2020, www.nytimes.com/2020/06/24/technology/facial-recognition-arrest.html

48. *Mass Incarceration Book* - Alexander, Michelle. The New Jim Crow: Mass Incarceration in the Age of Colorblindness. New York: New Press, 2010

49. *Media Literacy Organization* - "About." National Association for Media Literacy Education, 20 Feb. 2024, namle.org/about/

50. *Tree Octopus Hoax* - zapatopi.net/treeoctopus/

51. *Media Literacy Resources* - "Media Literacy Resources." California Department of Education, 16 Apr. 2024, www.cde.ca.gov/Ci/cr/ml/index.asp

52. *Digital Literacy Textbook* - LaGarde, Jennifer, and Darren Hudgins. Developing Digital Detectives: Essential Lessons for Discerning Fact from Fiction in the 'Fake News' Era. International Society for Technology in Education, 2021

53. *Education Statistics* - National Center for Education Statistics. National Center for Education Statistics, 2022

Chapter 6

54. *Student Privacy Law* - Barnett, Laura C. "The Protection of Pupil Rights Amendment (PPRA): A Guide for School Psychologists." NASP Communicator, vol. 49, no. 2, 2020, pp. 122-128. America First Legal Foundation, 19 May

2024, aflegal.org/wp-content/uploads/2022/09/Protection-of-Pupil-Rights-Amendment.pdf

55. *Testing Companies* - "Testing - The Testing Industry's Big Four." FRONTLINE, PBS, 1 Apr. 2024, www.pbs.org/wgbh/pages/frontline/shows/schools/testing/companies.html

56. *Special Education Law* - www2.ed.gov/parents/needs/speced/iepguide/index.html

57. *AI Institutional* Change- Gebru, Timnit. "Timnit Gebru: Ethical AI Requires Institutional and Structural Change." Stanford University, Human-Centered AI Institute, hai.stanford.edu/news/timnit-gebru-ethical-ai-requires-institutional-and-structural-change. Accessed 2 June 2024.

58. *AI Ethics Scenarios* - "Practicing AI Ethics Literacy: 10 Scenarios for Engaging with AI Ethics in Education." Institute for Ethics in Artificial Intelligence, Technical University of Munich, 5 Apr. 2024, www.ieai.sot.tum.de/practicing-ai-ethics-literacy-10-scenarios-for-engaging-with-ai-ethics-in-education/

59. *Educational Software* - "About Solve in Time!" Solve in Time!, 8 Apr. 2024, solveintime.com/home/about/

60. *GitHub Introduction* - "An Introduction to GitHub." Digital.gov, 29 Mar. 2024, digital.gov/resources/an-introduction-github/

Chapter 7

61. *AI Governance Lessons* - Lohr, Steve. "Let's Not Make the Same Mistakes with AI That We Made with Social Media." MIT Technology Review, 13 Mar. 2024,

www.technologyreview.com/2024/03/13/1089729/lets-not-make-the-same-mistakes-with-ai-that-we-made-with-social-media

62. *Solution Quote*- Norman, Donald A. The Design of Everyday Things. MIT Press, 2013.

63. *Forgetting Curve Study* - Murre, Jaap M., and Joeri Dros. "Replication and Analysis of Ebbinghaus' Forgetting Curve." PLoS ONE, vol. 10, no. 7, 2015, pp. 1-23. PubMed Central, doi.org/10.1371/journal.pone.0120644

64. *Liberatory Design* – "Liberatory Design — National Equity Project." National Equity Project, 2 Apr. 2024, www.nationalequityproject.org/frameworks/liberatory-desig

65. *Solve in Time* - "Home." Solve in Time!, 8 Apr. 2024, solveintime.com/home/

66. *Design Thinking Explanation* - Michelman, Paul. "Design Thinking, Explained." MIT Sloan Ideas Made to Matter, 30 Mar. 2024, mitsloan.mit.edu/ideas-made-to-matter/design-thinking-explained.

67. *AI Ethics Funding* - Baker, Dylan, and Alex Hanna. "AI Ethics Are in Danger. Funding Independent Research Could Help." Stanford Social Innovation Review, 29 Mar. 2024, ssir.org/articles/entry/ai_ethics_are_in_danger_funding_independent_research_could_help#

68. *Dr. John Wooden Quote* - Hill, Andrew. Be Quick- But Don't Hurry. Simon and Schuster, 2003.

Endnotes

About The Authors

Dee Lanier is the Lead Education Experience Designer at Lanier Learning, LLC and is an Education Coach for Samsung. Dee is dedicated to co-designing equitable learning experiences for school leaders, staff, and students. Lanier Learning also partners with nonprofit and for-profit corporations that are committed to community good. Dee is a passionate and energetic educator and learner with over two decades of instructional experience on the K-12 and collegiate levels. Dee holds Undergraduate and Master's degrees in Sociology with special interests in education, race relations, and equity. Dee is an award-winning presenter, TEDx Speaker, author of *Demarginalizing Design* and creator of the design thinking educational activities called, *Solve in Time!*® and *Maker Kitchen*™. Dee is also the co-host of *The Liberated Educator* podcast. Dee practices self-care by reading, playing percussion, and roasting, brewing, and drinking coffee. More information about Dee can be found at lanierlearning.com.

 Ken Shelton is a multi-award-winning educator with a Master's in Education (Educational Technology and New Media Design and Production), has dedicated over two decades to teaching and advancing educational technology. His expertise in educational leadership, organizational change, equity, and inclusion have earned him global recognition as a thought leader and highly sought after keynote speaker. Ken's contributions and extraordinary commitment to advancing digital learning experiences have garnered advisory roles for various organizations both public and private, shaping the future of education and technology worldwide. Recognized by leading educational institutions and publications for his unparalleled dedication to creating equitable and inclusive learning environments, Ken continues to make a significant impact in the field through his speaking engagements, trainings, and consultancy work. He is currently the Founder and CEO of Elevate Education. More information about Ken can be found at kennethshelton.net.

www.ingramcontent.com/pod-product-compliance
Lightning Source LLC
Chambersburg PA
CBHW080755120626
46557CB00006B/1275